The Barretts of Wimpole Stree

A Comedy in Five Acts.

Rudolf Wilhelm Besier was born in Blitar, East Java, in the Dutch East Indies,on July 2nd, 1878.

His father, the Dutch soldier Rudolf Wilhelm Besier, died whilst his mother, Margaret Ann Collinson, was pregnant with him. He was given his father's name in respect and remembrance.

As a playwright his early career, which began with The Virgin Goddess in 1906, was somewhat limited. In 1912 he worked with HG Wells to turn Kipps into a stage play and after the war with Hugh Walpole on Robin's Father. Other plays were produced but received little attention.

His great success came only in 1930. The Barretts of Wimpole Street was based on Elizabeth Barrett and Robert Browning's courtship. It was rejected by two London producers but did get to premiere at the Malvern Festival of 1930, produced by Sir Barry Jackson. (The first Malvern Drama Festival took place in 1929 dedicated to Bernard Shaw, six Shaw plays have debuted at Malvern including the 1929 English première of The Apple Cart, and the world première of Geneva in 1938).

Alas, American producers were not at all interested. Twenty seven were approached and 27 rejected it. The actress Katharine Cornell however staged at the Hanna Theatre in Cleveland in 1931, and then New York where it opened on February 9th, 1931 at the Empire Theatre, starring Katharine Cornell and Brian Aherne.

The Barretts of Wimpole Street became a major theatrical success and was turned, in 1934, into a glossy MGM film, starring Fredric March, Norma Shearer and Charles Laughton. The play was later used as the basis for a 1964 musical Robert and Elizabeth.

Rudolf Besier died in Surrey on June 16th, 1942, at the age of 63.

Index of Contents
ORIGINAL PRODUCTION
CHARACTERS OF THE PLAY
SCENE - Elizabeth Barrett's bed-sitting-room at 50, Wimpole Street, London, in 1845.
ACT I - Porter in a Tankard
ACT II - Mr. Robert Browning
ACT III - Robert
ACT IV - Henrietta
ACT V - Papa
Scene I
Scene II
RUDOLF BESIER – A CONCISE BIBLIOGRAPHY

ORIGINAL PRODUCTION

"The Barretts of Wimpole Street" was first produced at the Malvern Festival on August 20th, 1930, under the direction of Sir Barry Jackson.

The cast of the play was as follows:

Doctor Chambers	AUBREY MALLALIEU
Elizabeth Barrett Moulton-Barrett	GWEN FFRANGCON-DAVIES
Wilson	EILEEN BELDON
Henrietta Moulton-Barrett	MARJORIE MARS
Arabel Moulton-Barrett	SUSAN RICHMOND
Octavius Moulton-Barrett	BARRY K. BARNES
Septimus Moulton-Barrett	B. B. COLEMAN
Alfred Moulton-Barrett	HUGH MOXEY
Charles Moulton-Barrett	LEONARD BENNETT
Henry Moulton-Barrett	DOUGLAS QUAYLE
George Moulton-Barrett	ANTHONY MARSHALL
Edward Moulton-Barrett	CEDRIC HARDWICKE
Bella Hedley	JOAN BARRY
Henry Bevan	OLIVER JOHNSTON
Robert Browning	SCOTT SUNDERLAND
Doctor Ford-Waterlow	WILFRID CAITHNESS
Captain Surtees Cook	HARRY WILCOXON
Flush	TUPPENNY OF WARE

CHARACTERS OF THE PLAY

EDWARD MOULTON-BARRETT
ALFRED MOULTON-BARRETT
GEORGE MOULTON-BARRETT
CHARLES MOULTON-BARRETT
HENRY MOULTON-BARRETT
SEPTIMUS MOULTON-BARRETT
OCTAVIUS MOULTON-BARRETT
ARABEL MOULTON-BARRETT
HENRIETTA MOULTON-BARRETT
ELIZABETH
BARRETT MOULTON-BARRETT
ROBERT BROWNING
CAPTAIN W. SURTEES COOK
HENRY BEVAN
DOCTOR CHAMBERS
DOCTOR FORD-WATERLOWWATERLOW
BELLA HEDLEY

SCENE - Elizabeth Barrett's bed-sitting-room at 50, Wimpole Street, London, in 1845.

ACT I

PORTER IN A TANKARD

ELIZABETH BARRETT'S bed-sitting-room at 50, Wimpole Street, London. A window overlooking the street at the back. A door on the left. Fireplace on the right. It is best to give a description of the room in Elizabeth's own words from a letter to a friend:

". . . The bed like a sofa and no bed: the large table placed out in the room, towards the wardrobe end of it; the sofa rolled where a sofa should be rolled—opposite the armchair: the drawers crowned with a coronal of shelves (of paper, deal, and crimson merino) to carry my books; the washing-table opposite turned into a cabinet with another coronal of shelves; and Chaucer's and Homer's busts on guard over their two departments of English and Greek poetry; three more busts consecrate the wardrobe. . . . In the window is fixed a deep box full of soil, where are springing up my scarlet-runners, nasturtiums, and convolvuluses, although they were disturbed a few days ago by the revolutionary insertion among them of a great ivy root with trailing branches so long and wide that the top tendrils are fastened to Henrietta's window of the higher storey, while the lower ones cover all my panes. . . ."

It is evening; blinds and curtains are drawn; the fire glows dully; lamplight.

ELIZABETH lies on her sofa, her feet covered with a couvre-pied. Seated beside her is **DOCTOR CHAMBERS**, an elderly, white-whiskered man. He is feeling her pulse, watch in hand. **FLUSH**—Elizabeth's dog—lies asleep in his basket. On the table is a tray with the remains of a meal, and a pewter tankard.

CHAMBERS (dropping her wrist and pocketing his watch)
Hm—yes. It's this increasingly low vitality of yours that worries me. No life in you—none. . . . What are we going to do about it?

ELIZABETH (lightly)
Well, Doctor, if you shut a person up in one room for years on end, you can't very well expect to find her bursting with life and vigour! Why not prescribe something really exciting for a change?

CHAMBERS
Exciting, eh?

ELIZABETH
A gallop three times round the Park every morning—dumb-bell exercises—a course of callisthenics—a long sea-voyage . . .

CHAMBERS

How I wish I could, my dear!

ELIZABETH
It's funny to think of it now—but you know, Doctor, as a child I was a regular tom-boy!

CHAMBERS
Yes, I've heard all about that—and, mentally, you're a tom-boy still! To tell you the truth, Miss Ba—oh forgive me, my dear Miss Elizabeth, that quaint nickname of yours slipped out unawares! I'm always hearing it from your brothers and sisters. . . .

ELIZABETH (smiling)
Oh, please . . .

CHAMBERS
To tell you the truth, I'm not sure that brain of yours isn't altogether too active. The trouble with you is that you never will do anything in moderation—not even playing the invalid! Seriously, aren't we, perhaps, overdoing our studies?

ELIZABETH
Of course not.

CHAMBERS
Still hard at Greek?

ELIZABETH
Oh, not more than two or three hours a day.

CHAMBERS
Hm. Are you engaged on any literary work at the moment?

ELIZABETH
Only a few articles for the Athenæum and other papers.

CHAMBERS
The Athenæum—dear, dear! . . . Now why not give all these heavy labours a rest, and turn your mind to something light and easy for a change? . . . Poetry! You're not neglecting your poetry, I hope?

ELIZABETH
Meaning something—light and easy! (Laughs.) Oh Doctor, I must remember to tell that to Mr. Robert Browning when I see him to-morrow!

CHAMBERS
Robert Browning? A brother bard, eh?

ELIZABETH
Don't tell me you've never heard of him!

CHAMBERS

Well, my dear, poetry isn't much in my line, you know.

ELIZABETH

That's evident! All the same, read Mr. Browning's "Sordello"—and then come back and tell me that poetry's—light and easy!

CHAMBERS

I'll make a note of it. . . . Well, well, I suppose we mustn't rob you of your mental exercises if they keep you contented.

ELIZABETH

Contented! Oh Doctor, I shudder to think what my life would be like if I hadn't a turn for scribbling and study!

CHAMBERS

Hm, yes. Quite so. Yes. . . . And this isn't the liveliest house for anyone to live in—let alone an invalid.

ELIZABETH

No, I suppose not. . . . I wish dear Papa were a happier man! It would make such a world of difference to all of us. . . .

CHAMBERS

Happier, eh? It's no business of mine, but when a man has good health, plenty of money, and a jolly family of boys and girls, I can't see why he should make life a burden to himself and others! . . . It's amazing—incredible, and—well, as I said, it's no concern of mine. But you are, my dear—and a very worrying concern too! Of course, the winter has been abominable, and these spring months are always trying. The fact is you oughtn't to live in England at all. Italy's the place for you.

ELIZABETH

Italy! Oh Doctor, what a heavenly dream!

CHAMBERS

Yes—and must remain a dream, I fear. . . . But if only I could prescribe some sort of change for you—something—anything—to get you out of these dismal surroundings for a time. . . . Tell me now, Miss Elizabeth, have you ventured on your feet at all lately?

ELIZABETH

No, hardly at all. I rather lost my nerve after that fall I had last Christmas.

CHAMBERS

I remember.

ELIZABETH

Papa, as you know, or one of my brothers, carries me from my bed to the sofa in the morning, and back to bed again at night. Sometimes, when I'm feeling venturesome, my maid supports me across the room.

CHAMBERS

Feeling venturesome at the moment?

ELIZABETH
Not particularly. . . .

CHAMBERS
All the same, I think we'll try a step or two.

(Rising, he takes both of her hands.)

Quietly now—slowly—there's no hurry.

(With his assistance she gets on to her feet.)

There we are.

[She sways a little. He supports her.

Feeling giddy, eh?

ELIZABETH
A little. . . .

CHAMBERS
Close your eyes and lean against me. It will pass in a minute. . . . Better?

ELIZABETH
Yes. . . . Oh, yes. . . .

CHAMBERS
Take your time now, and step carefully. Don't be nervous; I won't let go your hands. . . .

(She takes a couple of faltering steps, he walking backwards holding her hands.)

No—don't look at the floor. Look straight ahead. . . . That's first rate—that's fine—splendid—splendid. . .

[After taking half a dozen steps she falters and sways.

ELIZABETH
Oh Doctor! . . .

(He quickly catches her in his arms and carries her back to the sofa.)

CHAMBERS
Feeling faint?

ELIZABETH
No, no, I'm all right. . . . I—I am really. . . . It's only my knees—they don't seem able to—to support me.

CHAMBERS

Well, if they can't do that, they're a pretty useless pair! Why, there's no more to you than to a five-year-old! . . . How's the appetite? Just peck at your food, I suppose?

ELIZABETH

I always try to eat what I'm given. But I'm never very hungry. (With sudden animation) Doctor, that reminds me! Do you remember Papa suggesting to you that a kind of beer—called porter—might do me good?

CHAMBERS

Yes—and an excellent suggestion too!

ELIZABETH

Oh, but forgive me, it was nothing of the kind! I have to drink it twice a day out of a pewter tankard—and my life, in consequence, has become one long misery!

CHAMBERS

God bless my soul!

ELIZABETH

I am not exaggerating—one long misery . . . !

CHAMBERS

But, my dear child, quite apart from its invaluable blood-making properties, porter is generally considered a most palatable beverage. There's nothing I enjoy more than a pint of porter with my steak or chops at breakfast.

ELIZABETH (in a shocked whisper)

With your breakfast! . . . All I can say is that to me porter is entirely horrible. . . . Horrible to look at, more horrible to smell, and most horrible to drink. Surely something one abominates so intensely can't possibly do one any good! It's no use my appealing to Papa—especially as the dreadful idea originated with him. But if you, dear, dear Doctor Chambers, were to suggest to him that something else—anything—I don't mind what it is—might be equally efficacious . . .

CHAMBERS (laughing)

You poor little lady! But of course I will!

ELIZABETH

Oh, thank you a thousand times!

CHAMBERS

What do you say to a couple of glasses of hot milk as a substitute?

ELIZABETH

I dislike milk—but I'll drink it all day long, if only you'll rescue me from porter!

[A knock at the door.

Come in.

[**WILSON**, **ELIZABETH'S** maid, enters. She is a fine, capable-looking girl in the middle twenties.

Yes, Wilson?

WILSON
Begging your pardon, Miss, but (turning to the **DOCTOR**) the Master wishes most particularly to see you before you leave, sir.

CHAMBERS
Of course, of course. . . .

(Looks at his watch)

And high time I were off! Is your Master in his study?

WILSON
Yes, sir.

CHAMBERS
Well, good-bye, Miss Elizabeth, good-bye.

(Takes her hand.)

ELIZABETH
Good-bye, Doctor. (In a low voice) And you won't forget?

CHAMBERS
Eh?

ELIZABETH (spelling the word)
P-O-R-T-E-R.

CHAMBERS (laughing)
I'll speak to him about it now.

ELIZABETH
Oh, thank you! thank you!

CHAMBERS (still laughing)
Good-night.

(To **WILSON**, as he goes to the door)

You needn't see me downstairs. I know my way.

WILSON
Thank you, sir.

[**DOCTOR CHAMBERS** goes out.

I'm just going to post your letters, Miss Ba. Shall I take Flush with me?

ELIZABETH (excitedly)
Quick, Wilson—away with it!

(Points at the tankard of porter.)

WILSON (bewildered)
What, Miss? . . .

ELIZABETH
I hadn't the courage to drink it at dinner. I was putting off the dreadful moment as long as I could. . . .

WILSON
Your porter, Miss?

ELIZABETH
And now dear Doctor Chambers tells me I needn't drink it any longer. Take it away! Quick! Quick! And never mention the word porter to me again!

WILSON
Lor', Miss! Very good, Miss. But since you haven't had your porter, won't you—

ELIZABETH (covering her ears)
I told you never to mention the word again! Take it away! Please! Please!

WILSON
Very good, Miss Ba. Come, Flush.

(She picks up the dog and puts him out of the room; then returns for the tray, with a rather concerned glance at **ELIZABETH**, who starts laughing.)

[**HENRIETTA** enters suddenly. She is a beautiful, high-spirited, blooming girl.

HENRIETTA
What are you laughing at, Ba?

ELIZABETH
Wilson thinks I've gone mad.

WILSON
Mad, Miss? What things you do say!

ELIZABETH (still laughing)
Will you, or won't you, take away that—that black beer?

WILSON
Very good, Miss.

[**WILSON** goes out.

HENRIETTA
I don't know why you're laughing, Ba, and you needn't tell me. Only don't stop! I'll tickle you if you think you can't keep it up without being helped! . . . Oh, dinner was awful!

ELIZABETH
But, Henrietta—

HENRIETTA
Awful! Awful!

ELIZABETH
Was Papa—

HENRIETTA
Yes, he was. It was awful. He was in one of his moods—the worst kind. The nagging mood is bad enough, the shouting mood is worse—but don't you think the dumb mood is the worst of all?

ELIZABETH
Yes, perhaps, but—

HENRIETTA
I don't believe there were more than a dozen remarks all through dinner—and most of them were frozen off at the tips! Papa would just turn his glassy eyes on the speaker. . . . You know? For the last twenty minutes or so the only sound in the room was the discreet clatter of knives and forks. Directly dinner was over he ordered his port to be taken to the study—and, thank Heaven! he followed it almost at once.

ELIZABETH
Doctor Chambers is with him now.

HENRIETTA
Oh Ba, I do hope, for all our sakes, his report of you isn't too good.

ELIZABETH
But, Henrietta . . .

HENRIETTA (all sudden contrition, kneeling at the sofa and putting her arms round **ELIZABETH**)
Forgive me, dearest! It was odious of me to say that! You know I didn't mean it, don't you? Nothing in the whole world matters to me if only you get better. You know that, don't you?

ELIZABETH

Of course I do, you silly child. But what you said makes Papa an inhuman monster. And that's wickedly untrue. In his own way—he cares for all his children.

HENRIETTA

In his own way . . . ! No dear, what I meant was that good news of any kind would be certain to aggravate him in his present mood. I don't know why it should, but it does. (With sudden anxiety) Ba, Doctor Chambers isn't dissatisfied with you? You're not worse?

ELIZABETH

No, no, dear; I am just the same—neither better nor worse. . . .

[**ARABEL** enters. She is a tall, dark, serious woman.

ARABEL

Oh, you're here, Henrietta! I've been looking for you everywhere. Papa has just sent you this note from his study.

HENRIETTA

Me? Oh dear! When he starts sending out notes from his study
look out for squalls!

(Opens the note and reads)

"I have heard this morning that your Aunt and Uncle Hedley, and your Cousin Bella, have arrived in London earlier than was expected. They are staying at Fenton's Hotel. Your cousin Bella and her fiancé, Mr. Bevan, propose to call on you to-morrow at 3 o'clock. You and Arabel will, of course, be here to receive them, and if Elizabeth is well enough, you will bring them upstairs to see her. I have written to invite your Uncle and Aunt and Cousin to dinner next Thursday.—Papa." Well!

ARABEL

I understand now why Papa seemed so—so displeased at dinner.

HENRIETTA

Vile-tempered you mean.

ARABEL

Is it necessary always to use the ugliest word?

HENRIETTA

Yes, Arabel—when you're describing the ugliest thing. Oh, but Papa is quite impossible! He got that letter from the Hedleys at breakfast. Why couldn't he have spoken then? Why couldn't he have spoken at dinner? Heaven knows he had opportunity enough!

ARABEL

I'm afraid he was too displeased.

HENRIETTA (with a grimace)

Displeased. . . . Oh, of course, we all know that he hates being ordinarily polite to anyone—and now he's simply bound to show some kind of hospitality to the Hedleys! No wonder he was—displeased.

ELIZABETH

Are you quite fair, dear? Papa seldom objects to us receiving our friends here.

HENRIETTA

For a cup of tea and a bun—and so long as the house is clear of them before he's back from the City! Has anyone of us ever been allowed to ask anyone to dinner? or even to luncheon? But that's an old story! What enrages me is that I was expecting a friend to-morrow at three—and now I shall have to put him off somehow.

ARABEL (archly)

Why?

HENRIETTA

Why what?

ARABEL (as before)

Why must you put your friend off? Bella and her fiancé won't eat—your friend.

HENRIETTA (angrily)

What—what business is that of yours?

ARABEL (dismayed)

But, Henrietta—

HENRIETTA

I hate people prying into my affairs! . . .

[She goes quickly out of the room, slamming the door behind her.

ARABEL (distressed)

Oh dear! Oh dear! What can be the matter with her to-night? Usually she quite enjoys being quizzed about Captain Surtees Cook.

ELIZABETH

Perhaps she may have begun to take his attentions seriously.

ARABEL

Oh Ba, I hope not! You remember when young Mr. Palfrey wanted to marry her two years ago—those dreadful scenes with Papa?

ELIZABETH

I should rather forget them.

ARABEL

Oh, why can't Henrietta realise that if there's one thing Papa will never, never permit, it's a marriage in the family? It doesn't worry me at all, as gentlemen never attracted me in that way. Nor you, dear.

ELIZABETH (with a laugh)
Me!

ARABEL
Of course, my poor darling, to-day anything of that kind is quite out of the question—Papa or no Papa. But even when you were younger and stronger, I don't ever remember your having had . . . little affairs with gentlemen.

ELIZABETH (whimsically)
Perhaps the gentlemen never gave me the chance.

ARABEL
Oh, but you were quite pretty as a young girl.

ELIZABETH
What is Captain Surtees Cook like? Is he nice?

ARABEL
Yes, I think so. Yes, quite nice. But he never says much. He just sits and looks at Henrietta.

ELIZABETH
She's very lovely. . . .

ARABEL
But Papa would never countenance any kind of understanding between them. Captain Cook would be forbidden the house at the least mention of such a thing—and it's dreadful to think what would happen to Henrietta! Even if he came offering her a coronet, instead of being an officer with a small allowance in addition to his pay, it would make no difference. You know that as well as I do.

ELIZABETH
Poor Henrietta. . . .

[**HENRIETTA** re-enters. She goes quickly up to **ARABEL** and kisses her.

HENRIETTA
I'm sorry.

ARABEL
Oh, my dear, I never meant to annoy you.

HENRIETTA
You didn't—you displeased me! (With a laugh) Oh, I'm Papa's daughter all right!

ELIZABETH
When Bella and her fiancé call to-morrow, Arabel will bring them up here to see me—and you can entertain Captain Cook in the drawing-room.

[**ARABEL** looks distressed.

HENRIETTA
What a thing it is to be a genius! You darling!

(Embraces **ELIZABETH**)

ELIZABETH
But I must have the room to myself at half-past three, as Mr. Robert Browning is calling then.

HENRIETTA (excitedly)
No!

ARABEL
But I thought—

HENRIETTA
Of course, I know you've been corresponding with Mr. Browning for months as I've posted any number of your letters to him. But then you write to so many literary people whom you absolutely refuse to see, and—

ARABEL
Has Papa given his permission?

ELIZABETH
Of course.

HENRIETTA
But why—why have you made an exception of Mr. Browning? I've heard he's wonderfully handsome, but—

ELIZABETH (laughing)
Oh, Henrietta, you're incorrigible!

ARABEL
I know he's been most anxious to call. Mr. Kenyon told me so.

HENRIETTA
But you said yourself, only a short time ago, that you didn't intend to receive him!

ELIZABETH
I didn't—and I don't particularly want to now.

HENRIETTA
But why?

ELIZABETH (lightly)
Because, my dear, at heart I'm as vain as a peacock! . . . You see, when people admire my work they are quite likely to picture the poetess as stately and beautiful as her verses. At least, that's what I always tell myself. . . . And it's dreadfully humiliating to disillusion them!

HENRIETTA
Don't be silly, Ba. You're very interesting and picturesque.

ELIZABETH (laughing)
Isn't that how guidebooks usually describe a ruin?

HENRIETTA
Oh Ba, I didn't mean—

ELIZABETH
Of course not, dear! . . . As a matter of fact, Mr. Browning has been so insistent that, out of sheer weariness, I've given way. But I don't want an audience to witness the tragedy of his disillusionment! So mind, Arabel—Bella and her Mr. Bevan must have left the room before he arrives.

[A knock at the door.

Come in.

[**OCTAVIUS BARRETT** enters. He is about eighteen, and he stammers slightly.

Come in, Occy.

OCTAVIUS
I've j-just come to see how you are, and to wish you g-good-night.

(Bends down and kisses her.)

Doctor satisfied?

ELIZABETH
Oh yes, I think so.

HENRIETTA (handing **OCTAVIUS** Barrett's note)
Read that, Octavius.

ARABEL (while **OCTAVIUS** reads)
Oh dear! I quite forgot that I was to attend a lecture on the Chinese Wesleyan Mission at Exeter Hall to-morrow afternoon!

OCTAVIUS

Well, you can't attend it.

(Flourishes Barrett's letter.)

This is undoubtedly a Royal D-decree!

HENRIETTA (dramatically)
Given at Our study at 50, Wimpole Street, on this 19th day of May, 1845. God save Papa!

ARABEL (reprovingly)
Henrietta dear!

[A knock at the door.

ELIZABETH
Come in.

[**SEPTIMUS BARRETT** enters. He is a year older than **OCTAVIUS**. Like **OCTAVIUS** and the other Barrett brothers who subsequently appear, he is in evening dress.

Well, Septimus?

SEPTIMUS
How are you, Ba? (Kisses her.) I hope the Doctor is satisfied with you?

ELIZABETH
Oh yes, I think so.

OCTAVIUS
I say, Septimus, the Hedleys are d-dining here in force next Thursday.

SEPTIMUS
Bai Jove! Not really?

[A knock at the door.

ELIZABETH
Come in.

[**ALFRED BARRETT** enters. He is older than **SEPTIMUS**.

Come in, Alfred.

ALFRED
And how's our dear Ba to-night? I hope the Doctor was happy
about you?

ELIZABETH

Oh yes, I think so.

[A knock at the door.

Come in.

[**CHARLES BARRETT** enters. He is somewhat older than ALFRED.

Come in, Charles.

CHARLES
How are you feeling to-night, Ba?

(Kisses her.)

I hope Doctor Chambers' report was good?

ELIZABETH
Oh yes, I think so.

[A knock at the door.

Come in.

[**HENRY BARRETT** enters. He is slightly older than **CHARLES**.

Come in, Henry.

HENRY
Well, Ba? How are you, my dear?

(Kisses her.)

Was the Doctor pleased with his patient?

ELIZABETH
Oh yes, I think so.

HENRY
That's good. I must say I think you are looking a little better. What d'you say, Charles?

CHARLES
Eh?

HENRY
Looking better, don't you know. More herself, what?

[A knock at the door.

ELIZABETH
Come in.

[**GEORGE BARRETT** enters. He is slightly older than **HENRY**.

Come in, George.

GEORGE
Well, and how's Ba to-night?

(Kisses her.)

The Doctor's just been, hasn't he? I'm afraid he wasn't too pleased with you.

ELIZABETH
Oh yes, I think so. . . . I mean—why?

GEORGE
You're not looking so well. Is she, Henry?

HENRY
On the contrary, I think she's looking considerably better. So does Charles. Don't you, Charles?

CHARLES
Eh?

OCTAVIUS
I say, George, the Hedleys have arrived unexpectedly in town. Bella and her swain are c-calling on the girls to-morrow afternoon. And on Thursday she and her parents are d-dining here in state.

ALFRED, HENRY, SEPTIMUS (simultaneously)
Dining here!

GEORGE
Well, I hope they'll enjoy their dinner as much as we did to-night!

HENRY
You have met this Mr. Bevan, haven't you?

GEORGE
I have.

HENRY
What is he like?

GEORGE
Pompous ass. But warm—a very warm man. Ten thousand pounds a year, if he has a penny.

HENRIETTA
No!

GEORGE
And ten thousand more when his grandmother dies.

ARABEL
Oh!

HENRIETTA
It's grossly unfair! What has Bella done to deserve such luck?

OCTAVIUS
George says he's a p-pompous ass.

HENRIETTA
Oh, that's jealousy! No man with ten thousand a year can be (imitating his stammer) a—p-p-p-p-pompous ass!

GEORGE
I think it's just possible that you'll all be interested to hear that Papa is going to Plymouth on business next week, and—

[Excited exclamations from all except **ELIZABETH**

HENRIETTA
Go on, George, go on! And—?

GEORGE
And that he's not expected to return—for at least a fortnight.

[Murmurs of satisfaction and smiling faces.

HENRIETTA
Oh, George!

(She flings her arms round his neck.)

How wonderful! How glorious! Do you polk, George?

GEORGE
Don't be childish.

HENRIETTA
Well, I polk!

[She dances the polka round the room, humming a polka measure. The others look on amused. **OCTAVIUS** claps his hands. The door is opened quietly and **EDWARD MOULTON-BARRETT** enters. He is a well-set-up handsome man of sixty.

ELIZABETH
Papa . . .

[An uneasy silence falls. **HENRIETTA**, in the middle of the room, stops dead. **BARRETT** stands for a moment just beyond the threshold looking before him with a perfectly expressionless face.

Good evening, Papa. . . .

[Without replying, **BARRETT** crosses the room and takes his stand with his back to the fireplace. A pause. No one moves.

BARRETT (in a cold, measured voice)
I am most displeased. (A pause.) It is quite in order that you should visit your sister of an evening and have a few quiet words with her. But I think I have pointed out, not once, but several times, that, in her very precarious state of health, it is inadvisable for more than three of you to be in her room at the same time. My wishes in this matter have been disregarded—as usual. (A pause.) You all know very well that your sister must avoid any kind of excitement. Absolute quiet is essential, especially before she retires for the night. And yet I find you romping around her like a lot of disorderly children. . . . I am gravely displeased.

[**HENRIETTA** gives a nervous little giggle.

I am not aware that I have said anything amusing, Henrietta?

HENRIETTA
I—I beg your pardon, Papa.

BARRETT
And may I ask what you were doing as I came into the room?

HENRIETTA
I was showing Ba how to polk.

BARRETT
To . . . polk?

HENRIETTA
How to dance the polka.

BARRETT
I see.

[A pause.

OCTAVIUS (nervously)
Well, B-Ba, I think I'll say g-good-night, and—

BARRETT
I should be grateful if you would kindly allow me to finish speaking.

OCTAVIUS
Sorry, sir. I—I thought you'd d-done.

BARRETT (with frigid anger)
Are you being insolent, sir?

OCTAVIUS
N-no indeed, sir—I assure you, I—

BARRETT
Very well. Now—

ELIZABETH (quickly, nervously)
As I am really the cause of your displeasure, Papa, I ought to tell you that I like nothing better than a—a little noise occasionally. (A slight pause.) It—it's delightful having all the family here together—and can't possibly do me any harm....

BARRETT
Perhaps you will forgive my saying, Elizabeth, that you are not the best judge of what is good or bad for you. . . . And that brings me to what I came here to speak to you about. Doctor Chambers told me just now that you had persuaded him to allow you to discontinue drinking porter with your meals.

ELIZABETH
It needed very little persuasion, Papa. I said I detested porter, and he agreed at once that I should take milk instead.

BARRETT
I questioned him closely as to the comparative strength-giving values of porter and milk, and he was forced to admit that porter came decidedly first.

ELIZABETH
That may be, Papa. But when you dislike a thing to loathing, I don't see how it can do you any good.

BARRETT
I said just now that you are not the best judge of what is good or bad for you, my child. May I add that self-discipline is always beneficial, and self-indulgence invariably harmful?

ELIZABETH
If you think my drinking milk shows reckless self-indulgence, Papa, you're quite wrong. I dislike it only less than porter.

BARRETT

Your likes and dislikes are quite beside the point in a case like this.

ELIZABETH
But Papa—

BARRETT
Believe me, Elizabeth, I have nothing but your welfare at heart when I warn you that if you decide to discontinue drinking porter, you will incur my grave displeasure.

ELIZABETH (indignantly)
But—but when Doctor Chambers himself—

BARRETT
I have told you what Doctor Chambers said.

ELIZABETH
Yes, but—

BARRETT
Did you drink your porter at dinner?

ELIZABETH
No.

BARRETT
Then I hope you will do so before you go to bed.

ELIZABETH
No, Papa, that's really asking too much! I—I can't drink the horrible stuff in cold blood.

BARRETT
Very well. Of course, I have no means of coercing you. You are no longer a child. But I intend to give your better nature every chance of asserting itself. A tankard of porter will be left at your bedside. And I hope that to-morrow you will be able to tell me that—you have obeyed your Father.

ELIZABETH
I am sorry, Papa—but I shan't drink it.

BARRETT (to **HENRIETTA**)
Go down to the kitchen and fetch a tankard of porter.

HENRIETTA
No.

BARRETT
I beg your pardon?

HENRIETTA (her voice trembling with anger and agitation)

It's—it's sheer cruelty. You know how Ba hates the stuff. The Doctor has let her off. You're just torturing her because you—you like torturing.

BARRETT
I have told you to fetch a tankard of porter from the kitchen.

HENRIETTA
I won't do it.

BARRETT
Must I ask you a third time? (Suddenly shouting) Obey me this instant!

ELIZABETH (sharply)
Papa . . . Go and fetch it, Henrietta! Go at once! I can't stand this. . . .

HENRIETTA
No, I—

ELIZABETH
Please—please . . .

[After a moment's indecision, **HENRIETTA** turns and goes out.

BARRETT (quietly, after a pause)
You had all better say good-night to your sister.

ARABEL (in a whisper)
Good-night, dearest.

(She kisses **ELIZABETH** on the cheek.)

ELIZABETH (receiving the kiss impassively)
Good-night.

[**ARABEL** leaves the room. Then each of the brothers in turn goes to **ELIZABETH** and kisses her cheek.

GEORGE
Good-night, Ba.

ELIZABETH
Good-night.

[**GEORGE** goes out.

ALFRED
Good-night, Ba.

ELIZABETH

Good-night.

[**ALFRED** goes out.

HENRY
Good-night, Ba.

ELIZABETH
Good-night.

[**HENRY** goes out.

CHARLES
Good-night, Ba.

ELIZABETH
Good-night.

[**CHARLES** goes out.

SEPTIMUS
Good-night, Ba.

ELIZABETH
Good-night.

[**SEPTIMUS** goes out.

OCTAVIUS
G-good-night, Ba.

ELIZABETH
Good-night.

[**OCTAVIUS** goes out.

BARRETT, standing before the fireplace, and **ELIZABETH** on her sofa, look before them with expressionless faces. A pause. **HENRIETTA** enters with a tankard on a small tray. She stands a little beyond the threshold glaring at her father and breathing quickly.

ELIZABETH
Give it to me, please.

[**HENRIETTA** goes to her. **ELIZABETH** takes the tankard, and is putting it to her lips, when **BARRETT** suddenly, but quietly, intervenes.

BARRETT
No.

(Putting **HENRIETTA** aside, he takes the tankard from **ELIZABETH** . To **HENRIETTA**)

You may go.

HENRIETTA
Good-night, Ba darling.

(She moves forward to **ELIZABETH**, but **BARRETT** waves her back.)

BARRETT
You may go.

ELIZABETH
Good-night.

[**HENRIETTA**, with a defiant look at her father, goes out.

BARRETT puts the tankard on the mantelpiece; then goes to the sofa and stands looking down at **ELIZABETH** . She stares up at him with wide, fearful eyes.

BARRETT (in a gentle voice)
Elizabeth.

ELIZABETH (in a whisper)
Yes?

BARRETT (placing his hand on her head and bending it slightly back)
Why do you look at me like that, child? . . . Are you frightened?

ELIZABETH (as before)
No.

BARRETT
You're trembling. . . . Why?

ELIZABETH
I—I don't know.

BARRETT
You're not frightened of me?

(**ELIZABETH** is about to speak—he goes on quickly)

No, no. You mustn't say it. I couldn't bear to think that.

(He seats himself on the side of the sofa and takes her hands.)

You're everything in the world to me—you know that. Without you I should be quite alone—you know that too. And you—if you love me, you can't be afraid of me. For love casts out fear. . . . You love me, my darling? You love your father?

ELIZABETH (in a whisper)
Yes.

BARRETT (eagerly)
And you'll prove your love by doing as I wish?

ELIZABETH
I don't understand. I was going to drink—

BARRETT (quickly)
Yes—out of fear, not love. Listen, dear. I told you just now that if you disobeyed me you would incur my displeasure. I take that back. I shall never, in any way, reproach you. You shall never know by deed or word, or hint, of mine how much you have grieved and wounded your father by refusing to do the little thing he asked. . . .

ELIZABETH
Oh please, please, don't say any more. It's all so petty and sordid. Please give me the tankard.

BARRETT (rising)
You are acting of your own free will, and not—

ELIZABETH
Oh, Papa, let us get this over and forget it! I can't forgive myself for having made the whole house miserable over a tankard of porter.

(He gives her the tankard.)

[She drinks the porter straight off. **BARRETT** places the tankard back on the mantelpiece; then returns to the sofa and looks yearningly down at **ELIZABETH.**

BARRETT
You're not feeling worse to-night, my darling?

ELIZABETH (listlessly)
No, Papa.

BARRETT
Just tired?

ELIZABETH
Yes . . . just tired.

BARRETT
I'd better leave you now. . . . Shall I say a little prayer with you before I go?

ELIZABETH
Please, Papa.

[**BARRETT** kneels down beside the sofa, clasps his hands, lifts his face, and shuts his eyes. **ELIZABETH** clasps her hands, but keeps her eyes wide open.

BARRETT
Almighty and merciful God, hear me, I beseech Thee, and grant my humble prayer. In Thine inscrutable wisdom Thou hast seen good to lay on Thy daughter Elizabeth grievous and heavy afflictions. For years she hath languished in sickness; and for years, unless in Thy mercy Thou take her to Thyself, she may languish on. Give her to realise the blessed word that Thou chastisest those whom Thou lovest. Give her to bear her sufferings in patience. Give her to fix her heart and soul on Thee and on that Heavenly Eternity which may at any moment open out before her. Take her into Thy loving care to-night; purge her mind of all bitter and selfish and unkind thoughts; guard her and comfort her. These things I beseech Thee for the sake of Thy dear Son, Jesus Christ. Amen.

ELIZABETH
Amen.

BARRETT (rising to his feet, and kissing her forehead)
Good-night, my child.

ELIZABETH (receiving his kiss impassively)
Good-night, Papa.

[**BARRETT** goes out.

ELIZABETH lies motionless staring before her for a moment or two. A knock at the door.

Come in.

[**WILSON** enters carrying **FLUSH**.

WILSON (putting **FLUSH** in his basket)
Are you ready for your bed now, Miss Ba?

ELIZABETH
Oh, Wilson, I'm so tired—tired—tired of it all. . . . Will it never end?

WILSON
End, Miss?

ELIZABETH
This long, long, grey death in life.

WILSON
Oh, Miss Ba, you shouldn't say such things!

ELIZABETH
No, I suppose I shouldn't. . . . Did Flush enjoy his run?

WILSON
Oh yes, Miss.

(A short pause.)

ELIZABETH
Is it a fine night, Wilson?

WILSON
Yes, Miss, and quite warm, and there's such a lovely moon.

ELIZABETH (eagerly)
A moon! Oh, do you think I can see it from here?

WILSON
I don't know, I'm sure.

ELIZABETH
Draw back the curtains and raise the blind.

[**WILSON** does so; and moonlight, tempered by the lamplight, streams on **ELIZABETH'S** face.

WILSON
There you are, Miss! The moon's right above the chimleys. You can see it lovely!

ELIZABETH (dreamily)
Yes. . . . Yes. . . . Please put out the lamp and leave me for a little. I don't want to go to bed quite yet.

WILSON
Very well, Miss Ba.

[**WILSON** extinguishes the lamp and goes out.

ELIZABETH is bathed in strong moonlight. She stares, for a while, with wide eyes at the moon. Then her quickened breathing becomes audible, and her whole body is shaken with sobs. She turns over on her side and buries her face in her arms. The only sound is her strangled weeping as the Scene closes.

ACT II

MR. ROBERT BROWNING

The afternoon of the following day. The curtains are drawn aside, the blinds are up, and sunshine pours into the room. On a little table near **ELIZABETH'S** sofa is a tray, with an untouched sweet on it.

[**ELIZABETH** lies on the sofa, her couvre-pied over her feet. She is reading a small book with intense absorption; now and again running her fingers through her ringlets, or tossing them back from her face. **FLUSH** lies in his basket.

ELIZABETH (with puzzled emphasis):
"With flowers in completeness,
All petals, no prickles,
Delicious as trickles
Of wine poured at mass-time."

[A knock at the door. **ELIZABETH**, absorbed, takes no notice. She repeats, clutching her forehead:

"All petals, no prickles,
Delicious as trickles—"

[The knock repeated.

"Of wine—"

Come in. . . .

[**WILSON** enters.

Oh yes, Wilson . . . I'm quite ready for lunch.

WILSON (stolidly)
You've had your lunch, Miss Ba.

ELIZABETH
Oh yes, of course. . . . And I enjoyed it very much!

WILSON
You only picked at the fish, Miss Ba. An' I took away the best part of that nice chop. An' I see you haven't touched the pudding—cornflour blammonge, too, with raspberry jam.

ELIZABETH (wonderingly regarding the tray)
Oh. . . . Anyhow, it's too late now. . . .

(She once more plunges into her book.)

[**WILSON** carries out the tray and re-enters immediately, shutting the door after her.

WILSON (going to the mantelpiece and measuring out some medicine into a medicine glass)
And now, Miss Ba, if you're all nice and comfortable, I'll take Flush out for his airing.

[**ELIZABETH** , absorbed in her reading, takes no notice. **WILSON** holds the glass of medicine towards her.

Your physic, Miss Ba.

ELIZABETH (taking the glass, with her eyes still fixed on her book)
Thank you.

(With the glass in her hand she continues reading.)

WILSON (going to the window)
I think, p'raps, I'd better pull down the blind a bit. Too much sun isn't good for you, Miss. . . .

(She half draws down the blind.)

ELIZABETH (holding out the untouched glass, her eyes still on the book)
Thank you. . . .

WILSON
You haven't drunk it yet, Miss.

ELIZABETH
Oh. . . .

(She swallows the medicine and, with a little grimace, hands the glass back to **WILSON**.)

Please open the door, Wilson. I am expecting visitors this afternoon, and I want the room to be quite fresh for them. How I wish we could open the window!

WILSON (shocked)
Open the window, Miss Ba!

ELIZABETH (with a sigh)
Yes, I know it's strictly forbidden. . . .Well, open the door wide.

WILSON
I'd best cover you well up first of all.

(Fetches a rug.)

Visitors, Miss Ba? . . .

ELIZABETH (while **WILSON** covers her up to her chin)
Yes, my cousin, Miss Bella Hedley. I haven't seen her since she was a child—such a lovely slip of a child! And now she's just become engaged.

WILSON
Indeed, Miss. And is she bringing her young gentleman with her?

ELIZABETH
Yes.

[**WILSON** opens the door.

And Mr. Robert Browning is calling later.

WILSON
Indeed, Miss? The gentleman who's always sending you such lovely boukeys?

ELIZABETH
Yes.

(Starts reading again.)

WILSON
Sure you don't feel a draught, Miss Ba?

ELIZABETH (without looking up)
Quite, thanks.

WILSON
Hadn't you better keep your arms covered? These spring days the air is that treacherous.

ELIZABETH (to herself, with despairing emphasis)
No—it's quite beyond me! I give it up!

WILSON
Beg pardon?

ELIZABETH (speaking intensely)
Wilson.

WILSON
Yes, Miss.

ELIZABETH (as before)
Have you noticed anything—strange in me to-day?

WILSON
Strange, Miss?

ELIZABETH
Yes, strange. I mean—dull-witted—thick-headed—stupid—idiotic. . . .

WILSON
Lor'! No! P'raps a bit absent-minded like—but that isn't anything for you to worry about, Miss Ba.

ELIZABETH
Then you don't think I'm going—mad?

WILSON
Mercy on us! Mad!

ELIZABETH
Very well. But now, listen carefully and tell me what you make of this:—
(She reads)
"And after, for pastime,
If June be refulgent
With flowers in completeness,
All petals, no prickles,
Delicious as trickles
Of wine poured at mass-time,—
And choose one indulgent
To redness and sweetness:
Or if, with experience of man and of spider,
June used my June-lightning, the strong insect-ridder,
To stop the fresh film work,—why June will consider."

Well?

WILSON (enthusiastically)
I call that just lovely, Miss Ba!

ELIZABETH
But do you know what it means?

WILSON
Oh no, Miss.

ELIZABETH
Does it convey anything at all to your mind?

WILSON
Oh no, Miss.

ELIZABETH (with a sigh of relief)
Thank Heaven for that!

WILSON
But then po'try never does, Miss. Leastways, not real po'try, like what you make.

ELIZABETH (laughing)
But I didn't write that! It's by Mr. Browning.

WILSON

He must be a clever gentleman!

ELIZABETH
Oh yes! He's all that!

[**WILSON** has picked up **FLUSH**.

Well, Flush dear, are you going to behave nicely to-day?

(She holds out her arms for the dog and **WILSON** gives it to her.)

I shall ask Wilson for a full report when she gets home. (To **WILSON**) Where are you taking him to?

WILSON
Well, Miss, being so fine, I thought of a little walk in the Park.

ELIZABETH
Oh yes. And mind you notice the flowers! I shall want to hear all about them. The laburnum is over of course. But there ought to be still some pink May, and tulips, and wall-flowers. And perhaps some early roses. . . . Oh Flush, I'd give almost anything to be going with you instead of Wilson!

OCTAVIUS (outside)
May I c-come in?

ELIZABETH
Occy, dear!

[**OCTAVIUS** enters. **ELIZABETH** gives **FLUSH** to **WILSON**.

What on earth are you doing at home at this time of the day?

[**WILSON** goes out, carrying **FLUSH**.

OCTAVIUS
Papa's b-bright idea. Suggested I should take a half-holiday to help you feed and entertain the l-love-birds.

ELIZABETH (laughing)
But why? Henrietta and Arabel are socially quite competent. So am I.

OCTAVIUS
But you labour under the d-disadvantage of being all the same sex. Papa appears to think that at least one male B-Barrett ought to show up. He seems fully determined to do the p-polite thing by the Hedleys. And when Papa is fully d-determined on a thing, that thing is done. Or am I wrong?

ELIZABETH (sighing)

No—that thing is done. . . . But now—I want you to be diplomatic. Captain Surtees Cook is calling at the same time as Bella and Mr. Bevan. He's coming to see Henrietta. . . .

OCTAVIUS

Is he, by Jove! And won't the gallant fella rejoice when he finds Henrietta chaperoned f-four times over!

ELIZABETH

I've arranged for Arabel to bring Bella and Mr. Bevan up here to see me. You must come with them.

OCTAVIUS

Must I indeed? And why?

ELIZABETH

So that Henrietta may have Captain Cook to herself for a little while.

OCTAVIUS

Oh. Ah. Yes. Quite so. I see. . . . And you d-don't look in the least ashamed of yourself!

ELIZABETH

I'm not.

OCTAVIUS

But does it occur to you, my dear Ba, that we may be doing Henrietta an uncommonly b-bad turn by encouraging this b-budding romance?

ELIZABETH

Yes. But I think we ought to chance that. . . .

[He looks at her questioningly.

Occy, when you six boys wished me good-night yesterday, a queer thought came into my mind. You weren't alive at all—just automata.

OCTAVIUS

By Jove!

ELIZABETH

Like automata, you get up at half past seven every morning. Like automata, you eat your breakfasts. Like automata, you go to your work. Like automata, you return home. You dine like automata. You go to bed like automata.

OCTAVIUS

But I say—

ELIZABETH

And though she works on different lines, Arabel is just as automatic. You all seem to me to have cut out of life everything that makes life worth living—excitement, adventure, change, conflict, frivolity, love. . .

OCTAVIUS

We haven't cut 'em out, my dear! That operation was performed by dear P-Papa.

ELIZABETH

I know, but—

OCTAVIUS

Oh, I admit we're a pretty spineless lot! But what would you? We're none of us particularly g-gifted—and we're all of us wholly dependent on Papa, and must obey, or be broken. You're not c-counselling sedition?

ELIZABETH

No—but not resignation. Keep your souls alive. What frightens me is that you may become content with a life which isn't life at all. You're going that way—all of you—except Henrietta.

OCTAVIUS

And what does she get by t-trying to be herself? More kicks than ha'pence!

ELIZABETH

Yes—but being kicked keeps one alive! So don't let us do anything, just for the sake of peace and quiet, to hinder her little romance. Even if it should come to grief.

OCTAVIUS

It will.

ELIZABETH

Grief is better than stagnation.

OCTAVIUS

All very f-fine, my dear Ba—but what about you?

ELIZABETH

Me?

OCTAVIUS

Yes, you. We may all, with the possible exception of young Henrietta, be drifting with the stream. But I don't notice that you make much of a struggle against it. Where did that p-porter finally g-get to last night?

ELIZABETH (with a dreary little laugh)

Oh, but I don't count! I am quite out of it. You have your lives before you. My life is over.

OCTAVIUS

Rubbish!

[**HENRIETTA** enters.

HENRIETTA

Why, Occy, what are you doing here?

OCTAVIUS
Papa's n-notion. He somehow got wind that Surtees Cook was p-prowling around this afternoon and sent me home to head the f-feller off.

ELIZABETH
Occy!

HENRIETTA (in breathless consternation)
How did he hear? He couldn't have heard—(to **ELIZABETH**) unless you, or Arabel—

ELIZABETH
Occy, you idiot! No, dear—

OCTAVIUS
Sorry! My little joke, you know. . . .

HENRIETTA (hotly)
I hate you!

OCTAVIUS
Quite right too.

(Puts his arm around her.)

I repeat, I'm sorry. You may s-slap me if you like.

HENRIETTA (half mollified)
I've a good mind to.

OCTAVIUS (sitting down and drawing her on to his knee)
No, my che-ild, it's like this. His Majesty sent me home to represent His Majesty at the reception. I don't intend to leave Bella's side—not even when she and her beloved come up here to emb-brace Ba. Meanwhile you'll amuse Cook—j-just as you're amusing me now.

(Kisses her.)

In fact, we may take this as a l-little rehearsal.

HENRIETTA (jumping up from his knee)

Occy! how can you be so vulgar!

(She listens.)

What's that?

(Runs to the window.) Oh Ba, they've arrived! And in state! The Bevan family barouche, powdered footman and all!

[**OCTAVIUS** joins her at the window.

Look at Bella! What a gown! What a bonnet! Lovely! Oh, and Mr. Bevan's whiskers!

(Gestures round her chin.)

Aren't you green with envy, Occy?

OCTAVIUS
Positively verdant.

HENRIETTA (pushing **OCTAVIUS** to the door)
Go and help Arabel receive them. Off with you! Quick! I'll wait here till Captain Cook arrives. I'm going to let him in. And then you and Arabel can bring Bella and Mr. Bevan up here.

OCTAVIUS
All c-cut and dried, what? But I-look here—

HENRIETTA
Go along with you!

(Pushes him out of the room and shuts the door. Then runs again to the window and looks eagerly down into the street.)

What's the time?

ELIZABETH (smiling)
Five minutes past three.

HENRIETTA
Past three?

ELIZABETH
Past three.

HENRIETTA
I don't understand. . . . He said three. . . .

(With sudden anxiety)

Ba! To-day is Thursday, isn't it?

ELIZABETH
Yes, dear.

HENRIETTA (with a sigh of relief)
Oh . . .

(Turns again to the window)

I wish he were able to come in his uniform. That would take the curl out of Mr. Bevan's whiskers!

[**ELIZABETH**
laughs.

Oh, there he comes!

[She runs out of the room leaving the door open.

ELIZABETH
Please shut the door.

(But **HENRIETTA** has gone. **ELIZABETH** smilingly shrugs her shoulders, picks up her book and starts reading. After a moment one hears voices outside; then approaching footsteps. **OCTAVIUS** re-enters.)

OCTAVIUS
Are you ready to receive them?

ELIZABETH
Yes, quite. What are they like, Occy?

OCTAVIUS
Oh, she's a dream of l-loveliness! And he—isn't. . . .

[He goes out. A pause. The voices grow nearer. Then **BELLA HEDLEY** flutters in. She is an exquisitely pretty, exquisitely turned-out little creature, voluble, affected, sentimental, with a constitutional inability to pronounce her r's. She is followed by **ARABEL, MR. HENRY BEVAN**, and **OCTAVIUS. MR. BEVAN** is a model of deportment, inwardly and outwardly. He affects a magnificent Kruger beard, and his voice and manner are as beautifully rounded as his legs.

BELLA (ecstatically)
Cousin Elizabeth!

ELIZABETH (stretching out her hand)
Bella, dear. . . .

BELLA
Ba!

(Drops on her knees at the sofa and embraces **ELIZABETH**.)

Deawest Ba! After all these years! . . . But oh, my poor, poor Ba, how sadly you've changed! So pale, so fwagile, so etheweal!

ELIZABETH
And you, Bella, are even lovelier than you promised to be as a child.

BELLA
Flattewer! (She kisses **ELIZABETH**
'S hand, and still holding the
hand, rises to her feet.) You hear that, Ha'wy? This is my dear, dear
Ha'wy. Mr. Bevan—Miss Elizabeth Ba'wett.

BEVAN (bowing)
Delighted, Miss Barrett, charmed. . . .

BELLA (stretching out her free hand to **BEVAN**. He takes it)
No, no, Ha'wy, you must take her hand. . . . (Tenderly to **ELIZABETH**) Such a little hand! So fwail! So
spiwitual!

BEVAN (taking **ELIZABETH'S** hand and bowing over it)
And the hand that penned so much that is noble and eloquent! . . . I am honoured, Miss Barrett.

ELIZABETH
Thank you. And may I congratulate you?—both of you? I hope you will be very happy.

BEVAN
Thank you, Miss Barrett. I am indeed a fortunate man!

BELLA
Dear Ha'wy. Dear Ba.

ELIZABETH
But won't you sit down? . . .

[**BELLA**, **ARABEL**, and **BEVAN** seat themselves. **OCTAVIUS** stands near the window.

BELLA
I adore your poems, Ba—especially when dear Ha'wy weads them! He wead me "Lady Gewaldine's
Courtship" the day after we became engaged. He weads so beautifully! And he too adores your poems—
which ought to please you, as he is dweadfully cwitical!

BEVAN
Oh, come, come, my pet!

BELLA
Oh, but Ha'wy, you are! He doesn't quite appwove of even Mr. Alfwed Tennyson's poems.

ELIZABETH
Really, Mr. Bevan?

BEVAN

I have nothing against them as poetry, no indeed. Mr. Tennyson always writes like a gentleman. What grieves me, Miss Barrett, is that his attitude towards sacred matters is all too often an attitude tinged with doubt.

ARABEL

How sad. . . .

BEVAN

Sad indeed, Miss Arabel! and I grieve to say a very prevalent attitude among the younger men of to-day. Loss of faith, lack of reverence, and a spirit of mockery, seem to be growing apace. Of course, I am not alluding to Mr. Tennyson when I say this. His work is always reverent even when expressing doubt. Now your poems, my dear Miss Barrett, show no touch anywhere of these modern tendencies. There's not a line in one of them that I would disapprove of even dear Bella reading.

ELIZABETH

That—that's very satisfactory. . . .

BELLA

Dear Ha'wy is so fwightfully earnest!

BEVAN

Oh come, come, my pet. . . .

OCTAVIUS

I say, Mr. B-Bevan, you've not yet met my father, have you?

BEVAN

No, that pleasure is yet to come.

OCTAVIUS

I think you and he would g-get on famously together!

BEVAN

Indeed?

BELLA

Oh yes! for dear Uncle Edward is fwightfully earnest as well! Mamma has often told me so. . . . But there is one matter on which they are bound to differ. Like Mamma and Papa, dear Uncle Edward is a stwict Nonconformist, Ha'wy.

BEVAN (sadly)

Ah, ah, indeed. . . .

ELIZABETH

Then you are a member of the Church of England, Mr. Bevan?

BEVAN

I am indeed, Miss Barrett. Like Bella, I was brought up in Dissent. But Oxford changed all that. A dear friend of mine persuaded me to attend the services at St. Mary's, where Doctor Newman preaches, you know; and to study Pusey's works. . . . Two years ago I was received into the Church.

ARABEL (in a scared voice)
Pusey . . . Doctor Pusey. . . . But, Mr. Bevan, you're not—you're not—

BELLA
Oh, but he is, dear Awabel, and so am I! We're both Puseyites! Of course, dear Mamma and Papa were fwightfully distwessed about it at first, and feared my change of faith was entirely due to dear Ha'wy's influence. But in weality, I had long felt a lack of something in Nonconformity. . . . Don't you think it lacks something, dear Ba? Don't you feel it's a form of worship less suited to people in our walk of life than to the lower orders?

ELIZABETH (with a quickly suppressed little laugh)
No, I—I can't say it ever struck me quite like that. . . . But now tell me, dear, when is the wedding to be? Or am I being indiscreet?

BEVAN
Not at all, dear Miss Barrett, not at all. We—

BELLA (excitedly)
Oh, that weminds me! Where's dear Henwietta? . . . The wedding? Early in August.

(Looks round the room)

Where's Henwietta?

OCTAVIUS
At the moment she's d-downstairs entertaining a friend.

BELLA
Oh, I wanted to ask her—A fwiend? Not that tall gentleman we passed in the hall?

ELIZABETH
Yes, Captain Surtees Cook.

BELLA
Oh, in the Army? How thwilling! I thought his ca'wiage was militawy! So he's a fwiend of dear Henwietta?

ELIZABETH
Yes. . . . You wanted to ask Henrietta something?

BELLA
Oh, yes! Oh Ba, I do so want her to be one of my bwidesmaids! Do you think—

[**HENRIETTA** enters. She is visibly distraite. **BELLA** jumps to her feet.

Henwietta!

(Taking both her hands)

Henwietta darling, I was just saying—Oh, you must be one of my bwidesmaids! you simply must!

HENRIETTA
Bridesmaids? Oh yes—at your wedding. I should love to, Bella. It's sweet of you to ask me. And of course I will—if Papa—But I'm sure he won't mind. . . .

BELLA
Mind? Uncle Edward? Why should he mind?

HENRIETTA
No, no, I'm sure it will be all right. I don't see how he could possibly object.

BELLA
Object? But I don't understand! . . . Isn't she funny, Ba? You're only asked to be a bwidesmaid, darling—not a bwide!

HENRIETTA
Yes, I know, but—Oh, it's so hard to explain. . . .

BEVAN (gravely helpful)
Perhaps Mr. Barrett looks on bridesmaids as frivolous irrelevancies at so solemn a sacrament as marriage . . . ?

HENRIETTA
No, no, Mr. Bevan. It's not that. It's—(the words suddenly rush out) It's simply that nothing—nothing at all in this house must happen without Papa's sanction. You know he once owned slaves in Jamaica. And as slavery has been abolished there, he carries it on in England. I'm quite serious. We are all his slaves here.

ARABEL
Henrietta!

[**BEVAN** and **BELLA** look astonished and embarrassed.

HENRIETTA
Well, aren't we? Aren't we, Occy? Aren't we, Ba? We can't move hand or foot without his permission. We've got to obey his least whim and fall in with his moods—and they're as changeable as the weather! We haven't a soul of our own, not one of us . . . ! I tell you, Bella, it's more than likely that he'll refuse to let me be your bridesmaid, for no rhyme or reason—except that he's out of temper!

OCTAVIUS
I say, what about t-tea?

ARABEL (rising quickly)
Oh yes, yes!

HENRIETTA
Tea is quite ready. I'm sorry—I—I forgot to tell you.

OCTAVIUS
Good Heavens, let's h-hurry or Captain Cook will have swallowed it all!

(Crosses to the door and opens it.)

HENRIETTA
He's gone. . . .

(She moves to the window and stands there, her face half averted.)

BELLA
A wivederci, deawest Ba!

(Kisses her.)

It's been so lovely seeing you! May I come soon again? And next time I shall want you all to myself—without Ha'wy, I mean.

ELIZABETH
Come whenever you like, dear.

BEVAN
But why must I be excluded?

BELLA
Because I've heaps and heaps to tell dear Ba about a certain big, big man who might easily gwow conceited if he heard me!

BEVAN
Oh, come, come, my pet.

[**BELLA** takes **ARABEL**'S arm. **BEVAN** bows over **ELIZABETH'S** hand.

Good-bay, dear Miss Barrett.

ELIZABETH
Good-bye. It was nice of you to come and see me.

BEVAN
Not at all. I have long been looking forward to the honour of meeting you. Good-bay.

[**BELLA**, her arm still in **ARABEL**'S, kisses her hand to **ELIZABETH**.

BELLA
Au wevoir, darling!

ELIZABETH
Auf wiedersehen.

[**BELLA** and **ARABEL** go out.

BEVAN (turning and bowing at the door)
Good-bay.

ELIZABETH
Good-bye.

[**BEVAN** goes out. **OCTAVIUS**, turning at the door, bows to **ELIZABETH**, in imitation of **BEVAN**, and follows him. **ELIZABETH** smiles, and glances at **HENRIETTA**, who still stands with averted face at the window; then she takes up a book and starts reading. A pause. Suddenly **HENRIETTA** turns on her.

HENRIETTA (vehemently)
Well, why don't you say something?

ELIZABETH (coldly)
What do you want me to say?

HENRIETTA
Nothing. . . . Oh Ba, don't scold me!

(Goes to **ELIZABETH**, and sits on the floor beside her sofa.)

I know I deserve it. I have been dreadful. But I couldn't help it. I'm so miserable.

ELIZABETH (quickly)
Miserable, dear?

HENRIETTA
Yes—and so—so wildly happy! . . . Ba dear, may I tell you about it? I oughtn't to, I know. Because if it should ever come to anything, and Papa asks if you had any idea of what was going on, you'll have to lie—which you hate doing—or admit that you knew. And then he'd vent half his rage on you for not warning him in time.

ELIZABETH
Never mind, dear. Go on.

HENRIETTA
Surtees has just asked me to marry him.

ELIZABETH

Oh Henrietta! But—

HENRIETTA

And, of course, I accepted him—and said that I couldn't. And I had to tell him that we must never see each other again. When he calls here to-morrow, we shall have to—

ELIZABETH

You're not talking sense, child. What really has happened?

HENRIETTA

I don't know . . . except that we both love each other terribly. . . . Oh Ba, what are we to do? Surtees has only just enough money to keep himself decently. And, of course, I haven't a penny of my own. If only I had your four hundred a year, I might defy Papa and leave the house and marry Surtees to-morrow!

ELIZABETH

And what earthly good is that money to me? I'd give it to you, and how gladly—

HENRIETTA

I know you would, darling! But that's utterly impossible! Just think what your life would be like if Papa knew that you had made it possible for me to marry! No. But isn't it a cruel irony that the only one of the family with the means to be free and happy hasn't any use for it? (With sudden urgency) Ba dear, is there anything—anything at all—to be said for Papa's attitude towards marriage? Can it possibly be wrong to want a man's love desperately—and—and to long for babies of my own?

ELIZABETH

No. . . . But who am I to answer a question like that? Love and babies are so utterly remote from my life. . . .

HENRIETTA

Yes, I know, dear. You're a woman apart. But love and babies are natural to an ordinary girl like me. And what's natural can't be wrong.

ELIZABETH

No. . . . And yet the holiest men and women renounced these things. . . .

HENRIETTA

I daresay. But I'm not holy. And come to that neither is
Papa—not by any means! Didn't he marry, and—

[A knock at the door.

ELIZABETH

Come in.

[**WILSON** enters.

WILSON

Mr. Robert Browning has called, Miss.

ELIZABETH (breathlessly)
Mr.—Mr. Browning . . . ?

WILSON
Yes, Miss.

HENRIETTA
Then I'd better be off!

ELIZABETH (agitated. Quickly)
No—no, stay here. I can't see him. I—I don't feel up to it. I can't—

HENRIETTA
But Ba, what on earth is the matter? You told me yesterday—

ELIZABETH
I know. I know. But I really don't feel that I can see him now. (To **WILSON**) Tell Mr. Browning I am very sorry but I am not well enough to receive him.

HENRIETTA
But that's not true, Ba! You can't send him away like that, dear. It would be too rude and unkind after having asked him to call, and all the efforts he has made to get here. (To **WILSON**) Where is Mr. Browning?

WILSON
I showed him into the library, Miss.

ELIZABETH
But I—I'd much—much rather not see him. . . .

HENRIETTA
Oh fudge! You're not a silly schoolgirl! I'll bring him up myself. Mr. Kenyon says he's wonderfully romantic-looking, and quite the dandy.

[**HENRIETTA** goes out.

ELIZABETH
Is—is my hair tidy?

WILSON
Yes, Miss Ba.

ELIZABETH
Oh, please arrange the couvre-pied. . . .

[**WILSON** arranges the couvre-pied.

Thank you. . . . And, Wilson—no. . . . Thank you, that will do. . . .

WILSON
Yes, Miss.

(She goes out.)

[**ELIZABETH**, obviously in a state of strained nerves, awaits the coming of **ROBERT BROWNING**. A pause.

HENRIETTA enters.

HENRIETTA
Mr. Robert Browning.

[**ROBERT BROWNING** enters. He is a dark handsome man in the middle thirties, faultlessly, perhaps even a trifle foppishly, dressed. Over his shoulder he wears a cape fastened with a chain at the throat. He carries his high hat, lemon-coloured gloves, and clouded cane. **BROWNING'S** manner is sincere and ardent; his speech rapid, voluble, and emphasised by free gestures. **HENRIETTA** goes out.

BROWNING (pausing for a moment a few steps beyond the threshold)
Miss Barrett? . . .

ELIZABETH (stretching out her hand)
How-do-you-do, Mr. Browning?

BROWNING (quickly lays aside his hat, cane and gloves, and crossing to the sofa, takes her hand in both of his)

Dear Miss Barrett—at last!

(Raises her hand to his lips)

At last!

ELIZABETH (still all nerves, and rather overcome by the ardour and unconventionality of his manner) I— I've had to put off the pleasure of meeting you much longer than I wished. . . .

BROWNING (still holding her hand)
Would you ever have received me if I hadn't been so tiresomely insistent?

ELIZABETH
As you know from my letters, I've not been at all well during the winter, and I—

(Realising that her hand is still in his, she gently withdraws it.)

But won't you take off your cape?

BROWNING

Thank you.

(Unfastens his cape and lays it aside.)

ELIZABETH
I—I hope you don't find the room very close, Mr. Browning?

BROWNING
No, no. . . .

ELIZABETH
My doctor obliges me to live in what I am afraid must be to you a—a hot-house temperature. . . .

BROWNING (who has thrown a quick glance round the room)
Wonderful! You may think, Miss Barrett, that this is the first time I've been here. You're quite wrong, you know!

ELIZABETH
But—

BROWNING
Quite wrong. I have seen this room more times than I can remember. It's as familiar to me as my own little study at home! Before I came in, I knew just how your books were arranged, just how that tendril of ivy slanted across the window-panes—and those busts of Homer and Chaucer are quite old friends, and have looked down on me often before! . . .

ELIZABETH (smilingly protesting)
No, really—!

BROWNING
But I could never make out who the other fellows were on the top of the wardrobe, and—

ELIZABETH (laughing, and now quite at her ease)
Oh come, Mr. Browning! I know that dear Mr. Kenyon is never tired of talking about his friends; but I can't believe that he described my poor little room to you in detail!

BROWNING (seating himself beside her)
I dragged all the details I possibly could out of him—and my imagination supplied the rest. Directly after I had read your brave and lovely verses I was greedy for anything and everything I could get about you.

ELIZABETH (smilingly)
You frighten me, Mr. Browning!

BROWNING
Why?

ELIZABETH

Well, you know how Mr. Kenyon's enthusiasms run away with his tongue? He and I are the dearest of friends. What he told you about poor me I quite blush to imagine!

BROWNING
You mean, Miss Barrett, about you—you yourself?

ELIZABETH
I feel it would be hopeless for me to try to live up to his description.

BROWNING
He never told me anything about you—personally—which had the slightest interest for me.

ELIZABETH (puzzled)
Oh?

BROWNING
Everything he could give me about your surroundings and the circumstances of your life I snatched at with avidity. But all he said about you was quite beside the point, because I knew it already—and better than Mr. Kenyon, old friend of yours though he is!

ELIZABETH
But—Oh Mr. Browning, do my poor writings give me so hopelessly away?

BROWNING
Hopelessly—utterly—entirely—to me! . . . I can't speak for the rest of the world.

ELIZABETH (smilingly)
You frighten me again!

BROWNING
No?

ELIZABETH
But you do! For I'm afraid it would be quite useless my ever trying to play-act with you!

BROWNING
Quite useless!

ELIZABETH
I shall always have to be—just myself?

BROWNING
Always.

ELIZABETH
Oh . . . (quickly) And you too, Mr. Browning?

BROWNING

Always—just myself!

(He stretches out his hand; she takes it with a smile. Then, with a sudden laugh)

But really, you know, Miss Barrett, I shan't be able to take much credit for that! Being myself comes to me as easily as breathing. It's play-acting I can't manage—and the hot water I've got into in consequence . . . ! If life's to run smoothly we should all be mummers. Well, I can't mum!

ELIZABETH
Yes, I can well believe that now I know you. But isn't it extraordinary? When you are writing you never do anything else but—play-act.

BROWNING
I know—

ELIZABETH
You have never been yourself in any one of your poems. It's always somebody else speaking through you.

BROWNING
Yes. And shall I tell you why? I am a very modest man. (Quickly, after a slight pause) I am really!

ELIZABETH (with suppressed amusement)
I didn't question it, Mr. Browning.

BROWNING
So modest, I fully realise that if I wrote about myself—my hopes and fears, hates and loves, and the rest of it—my poems would be intolerably dull.

ELIZABETH (laughingly, vivaciously)
Well—since we are pledged to nothing but the truth, I won't contradict that—until I know you better!

BROWNING (with a laugh)
Bravo!

ELIZABETH (ardently)
Oh, but those poems, with their glad and great-hearted acceptance of life—you can't imagine what they mean to me! Here am I shut in by four walls, the view of Wimpole Street my only glimpse of the world. And they troop into the room and round my sofa, those wonderful people of yours out of every age and country, and all so tingling with life! life! life! No, you'll never begin to realise how much I owe you!

BROWNING (with emotion)
You—you really mean that?

ELIZABETH
Why, why, Mr. Browning—

BROWNING

But of course you do, or you wouldn't say it! And you'll believe me when I tell you that what you have said makes up to me a thousand times over for all the cold-shouldering I've had from the public?

ELIZABETH (fiercely)
Oh, it infuriates me! Why can we never know an eagle for an eagle until it has spread its wings and flown away from us for good? Sometimes—I detest the British public!

BROWNING (lightly)
Oh no, no! Dear old British public! At least it gives us generously the jolly pastime of abusing it! And mind you, Miss Barrett, I've an uneasy feeling that my style, is largely to blame for my unpopularity.

ELIZABETH (a little too eagerly)
Oh, surely not!

BROWNING
Didn't we agree never to play-act with each other?

ELIZABETH (with a laugh)
Touché! Well, perhaps, there are passages in your work a little invol—I mean a little too—too profound for the general reader.

BROWNING
Oh no! it's not what I say, but how I say it.

ELIZABETH
Oh, but—

BROWNING
And yet to me it's all simple and easy as the rule of three! And to you?

ELIZABETH
Well . . . not quite always. Sometimes there are passages. . . .

(She picks up a book.)

I have marked one or two in your "Sordello" which rather puzzle me. Here, for instance . . .

(She
opens the book and hands it to him.)

BROWNING (taking the book)
Oh, "Sordello"! Somebody once called it "a horror of great darkness"! I've done my best to forget it. However—

(He reads the passage to himself, smiling. The smile fades; he passes his hand over his brow and reads it again. She watches him, covertly smiling. He mutters)

Extraordinary. . . . But—but a passage torn from its context. . . .

[He rises and goes to the window, as though to get more light on the subject, and reads the passage a third time. **ELIZABETH** has some difficulty in suppressing her amusement. He turns to her with an expression of humorous chagrin.

ELIZABETH
Well? . . .

BROWNING
Well, Miss Barrett—when that passage was written only God and Robert Browning understood it. Now only God understands it.

[She laughs, and he joins in.

What do you say—shall we lighten this great darkness by pitching it on the fire?

ELIZABETH (indignantly)
No indeed! We shall do nothing of the kind! Please give me back the book.

[He does so.

Such passages are only spots on the sun. I love "Sordello."

BROWNING (eagerly)
You would! Of course you would! And shall I tell you why? Because it's a colossal failure.

ELIZABETH
If by a failure you mean an attempt—yes! you're right! That's just why "Sordello" appeals to my very heart. I too am always making colossal attempts—and always failing.

BROWNING
Isn't one such failure worth a hundred small successes?

ELIZABETH
Oh, a thousand and more!

BROWNING (eagerly)
You think so too? But, of course, I knew that! . . . Miss Barrett, you smiled when I told you that Kenyon had no need to describe you because I knew you through and through already. And what you have just said about success and failure proves to me finally how right I was. All Kenyon did was to fill in the background. I—I had painted the portrait—with the true soul of you, ardent and lovely, looking out of it.

ELIZABETH
Ardent and lovely! And you think you know me!

(With a bitter smile)

Oh, Mr. Browning—too often impatient and rebellious. . . .

BROWNING

Well, what of it? I've no love for perfect patience under affliction. My portrait is the portrait of a woman, not a saint. Who has more right to be impatient and rebellious than you?

ELIZABETH

Did Mr. Kenyon paint my background with a very gloomy brush?

BROWNING

Old Rembrandt would have envied him!

ELIZABETH (smilingly)

Poor dear Mr. Kenyon! He is more Royalist than the Queen herself! I assure you my afflictions worry him a great deal more than they worry me. . . . I suppose he told you that I am a—a dying woman?

BROWNING

We are all of us—dying.

ELIZABETH

And that our family life was one of unrelieved gloom?

BROWNING

Yes, he hinted at something of the sort.

ELIZABETH

He really shouldn't say such things! Frankly now, Mr. Browning, do you find me such a very pitiable object?

BROWNING

I find you, as I expected to find you, full of courage and gaiety. . . . And yet, in spite of what you say, I'm not at all sure that Kenyon's colours were too sombre.

ELIZABETH

But—

BROWNING (eagerly interrupting)

No, no, listen to me. Those colours are not yet dry. They must be scraped off! The whole background must be repainted! . . . And if only you'll allow it—I must have a hand in that splendid work.

ELIZABETH

But, Mr. Browning—

BROWNING (carried away)

No, listen! I'll dip my brush into the sunrise and the sunset and the rainbow! You say my verses have helped you—they're nothing. It's I—I who am going to help you now! We have come together at last—and I don't intend to let you go again.

ELIZABETH

But—

BROWNING
No, listen. Give me your hands.

(Bends forward and takes them.)

I've more life than is good for one man—it seethes and races in me. Up to now I've spent a little of all that surplus energy in creating imaginary men and women. But there's still so much that I've no use for but to give! Mayn't I give it to you? Don't you feel new life tingling and prickling up your fingers and arms right into your heart and brain?

ELIZABETH (rather frightened and shaken)
Oh please . . . Mr. Browning, please let go my hands. . . .

[He opens his hands; but she still leaves hers lying on his palms for a moment. Then she withdraws them, and clasping her cheeks, looks at him with wide, disturbed eyes.

BROWNING (softly)
Well?

ELIZABETH (a little shakily, with forced lightness)
You—you are really rather an overwhelming person, and in sober truth, I'm—

BROWNING
No—don't tell me again that you are afraid of me! You're not. It's life you're afraid of—and that shouldn't be.

ELIZABETH
Life?

BROWNING
Yes.

ELIZABETH
Well, when life becomes a series of electric shocks . . . !

BROWNING (smiling)
Was it as bad as all that?

ELIZABETH (smiling)
Indeed, yes! Do you affect other people in the same way?

BROWNING
They've often told me so.

ELIZABETH (lightly)

No wonder I hesitated about meeting you, much as I wanted to! Something of your disturbing vitality must have come to me from your letters and poems. . . . You'll laugh at me, Mr. Browning, but do you know we very nearly didn't meet to-day after all! When my maid told me you had arrived I was so panic-stricken that I all but sent down a message that I was too unwell to receive you. And it was a big effort to pull myself together, and behave like a sensible woman, when you came into the room!

BROWNING
I think I must have been quite as nervous as you at that moment.

ELIZABETH
You, Mr. Browning!

BROWNING
Yes—and I'm anything but a nervous man as a rule. But that moment was the climax of my life—up to now. . . . Miss Barrett, do you remember the first letter I wrote to you?

ELIZABETH
Yes indeed! It was a wonderful letter.

BROWNING
You may have thought I dashed it off in a fit of white-hot enthusiasm over your poems. I didn't. I weighed every word of every sentence. And of one sentence in particular—this sentence: "I love your books with all my heart—and I love you too." You remember?

ELIZABETH (lightly)
Yes—and I thought it charmingly impulsive of you!

BROWNING (almost with irritation)
But I tell you there was nothing impulsive about it. That sentence was as deeply felt and anxiously thought over as any sentence I've ever written.

ELIZABETH
I hope I have many readers like you! It's wonderful to think I may have good friends all the world over whom I have never seen nor heard of.

BROWNING
I am not speaking of friendship, but of love.

[**ELIZABETH** about to make a smiling rejoinder.

No, it's quite useless your trying to put aside the word with a smile and a jest. I said love—and I mean love—

ELIZABETH
But really, Mr. Browning, I must ask you—

BROWNING (swiftly interrupting her)

I'm neither mad nor morbidly impressionable—I'm as sane and level-headed as any man alive. Yet all these months, since first I read your poems, I've been haunted by you. And to-day you are the centre of my life.

ELIZABETH (very gravely)
If I were to take you seriously, Mr. Browning, it would, of course, mean the quick finish of a friendship which promises to be very pleasant to both of us.

BROWNING
Why?

ELIZABETH
You know very well that love—in the sense you, apparently, use the word—has no place, and can have no place, in my life.

BROWNING
Why?

ELIZABETH
For many reasons—but let this suffice. As I told you before, I am a dying woman.

BROWNING (passionately)
I refuse to believe it! For if that were so, God would be callous, and I know that He's compassionate— and life would be dark and evil, and I know that it's good. You must never say such a thing again. I forbid you to.

ELIZABETH
Forbid, Mr. Browning? . . .

BROWNING
Yes—forbid. Isn't it only fair that if you forbid me to speak of you as I feel, and I accept your orders, as I must, that I should be allowed a little forbidding as well?

ELIZABETH
Yes, but—

BROWNING (breaking in with sudden gaiety)
Dear Miss Barrett, what a splendid beginning to our friendship! We have known each other a bare half hour and yet we've talked intimately of art and life and death and love, and we've ordered each other about, and we've almost quarrelled! Could anything be happier and more promising? . . . With your permission, I'm going now. Mr. Kenyon impressed upon me to make my first visit as short as possible, as strangers tire you. Not that I'm a stranger!—still I can see that you are tired. . . . When may I call again?

ELIZABETH (a little dazed)
I don't quite know . . . I—

BROWNING
Will next Wednesday suit you?

ELIZABETH (as before)
Yes, I—I think so. But perhaps it would be better—

BROWNING
Next Wednesday then.

ELIZABETH
But—

BROWNING
At half past three again?

ELIZABETH
Yes—but I—

BROWNING (bowing over her hand)
Au revoir then.

ELIZABETH
Good-bye.

BROWNING (gently masterful, retaining her hand)
Au revoir.

ELIZABETH (a little breathlessly, after a slight pause)
Au revoir.

BROWNING
Thank you.

[He kisses her hand, turns and picks up his hat and cape, etc., and goes out. The moment after the door has closed behind him **ELIZABETH** sits up and clasps her face with both her hands. Then she slips off the sofa and unsteadily gets on to her feet. With the help of the table and the chairs, she manages to cross the room to the window. Grasping the curtain to support herself, she stands looking down into the street after the departing **BROWNING**, her face as alive with excitement and joy as though she were a young girl. And the Scene slowly closes.

ACT III

ROBERT

Some three months later.

DOCTOR CHAMBERS stands by the fireplace. **DOCTOR FORD-WATERLOWWATERLOW** sits on the sofa. He is a sharp-featured, sharp-tongued old man. Both **DOCTORS** are intently watching **ELIZABETH** as she walks with firm and sure tread across the room to the window and back again. **FLUSH** lies on the sofa.

FORD-WATERLOW
Once again, if you please.

[**ELIZABETH** walks across the room again.

My dear Miss Barrett, I congratulate you. Now sit down.

(She sits close to him, and he feels her pulse while talking.)

When exactly was it you last called me in for consultation, Doctor Chambers?

CHAMBERS
Three months ago almost to a day.

FORD-WATERLOW
Yes, yes—and your patient was in a very low condition at the time. Well, you've done wonders, Doctor.

CHAMBERS
Oh, mine was just the ordinary spade-work. Honesty compels me to give most of the credit to another.

FORD-WATERLOW
Eh?

CHAMBERS
The real healer is no one but Miss Barrett herself.

ELIZABETH
But, Doctor . . . !

CHAMBERS
I mean it, my dear, I mean it. Three months ago you seemed more than a little inclined to let life and the world slip through your pretty fingers. Then slowly the change began. Oh believe me, I was watching you like a lynx! Life and the world became more and more worth grasping. The wish to live is better than a dozen physicians—as I think even my distinguished friend will admit.

FORD-WATERLOW
The wish to live. . . . Hm, yes. . . . And you are able to get about and take the air occasionally nowadays?

ELIZABETH
Oh yes, Doctor. I have visited some of my friends, and been for several delightful drives round the Park. The only bother is getting up and down stairs. I'm inclined to lose my head going down, and I'm not yet able to undertake the upward journey.

FORD-WATERLOW
Quite so. Quite so.

CHAMBERS (smilingly)
Fortunately it doesn't need a very strong man to carry you.

ELIZABETH
Oh, but that's where you're wrong! (To **FORD-WATERLOW**) You have no idea how I am putting on weight!

FORD-WATERLOW
Is that so indeed?

CHAMBERS (solemnly)
So much so, that I have seriously thought of docking Miss Barrett's porter—a beverage, I may say, of which she is inordinately fond.

ELIZABETH (laughing)
I wonder you're not ashamed to mention that subject, Doctor Chambers!

FORD-WATERLOW
Well now, about the future, Miss Barrett. I fully agree with Doctor Chambers that another winter in London must, if possible, be avoided. If you continue picking up strength as you are doing, I see no reason against your travelling South by October, say.

ELIZABETH (with barely controlled eagerness)
Travelling . . . South? . . .

FORD-WATERLOW
To the Riviera, or, better still, to Italy.

ELIZABETH (breathlessly)
Italy . . . ! Oh, Doctor, do you really mean it?

FORD-WATERLOW
Why not? You could travel there by easy stages. I have been given to understand that you have set your heart on Italy, and that there are no—er—practical difficulties in the way of your going there.

ELIZABETH
If by practical, you mean financial—none at all. I have my own little income, and—

FORD-WATERLOW
Quite so, quite so.

CHAMBERS
I've taken the liberty to tell Doctor Ford-Waterlow of the only real difficulty in the way of your wintering abroad, and he is quite prepared to deal with—him.

FORD-WATERLOW
Quite—and drastically.

ELIZABETH (quickly)
Oh, I am sure that won't be necessary! Papa may not raise any kind of objection. It depends how he is feeling at the time, and—

FORD-WATERLOW (testily)
Fiddlesticks, my dear young lady! Mr. Barrett's feelings are neither here nor there. All that matters is his daughter's health and happiness, as I intend to make clear to him. Quite clear.

ELIZABETH
Oh, you mustn't think that Papa isn't kindness and generosity itself. But gentlemen have their moods. . . . Italy! Oh, it's hard to take in even the bare possibility of going there! My promised land, Doctor, which I never thought to see otherwise than in dreams!

FORD-WATERLOW (rising)
Well, well, let us hope realisation won't bring disillusion along with it! A grossly overrated country to my mind. Nothing but heaps of rubbish, dust, flies, stenches, and beggars! Good-bye, my dear Miss Barrett. No, please don't get up.

(Takes her hand.)

I'm delighted with your improvement. Delighted. And now for a little talk with your father. Good-bye.

ELIZABETH
Good-bye, Doctor.

CHAMBERS
Good-bye, Miss Elizabeth.

ELIZABETH
Good-bye.

[Both **DOCTORS** go out. **ELIZABETH** clasps her cheeks and whispers:

Italy—Italy—Italy. . . . (She picks up **FLUSH**) And you're coming with us, too, Flushy! We'll see Rome together, Florence, Venice, Vesuvius—

[**ARABEL** enters. **ELIZABETH** puts **FLUSH** down and jumps to her feet.

Arabel! (Embracing **ARABEL** impetuously) It's all but settled, my dear! I'm to go to Italy! He says that I shall be quite fit to travel by October! . . . Rome! Florence! Venice! Vesuvius! Raphael! Dante! "Sordello"! . . . Oh, I don't know what I'm saying—I'm quite off my head with excitement!

ARABEL
How wonderful for you! I'm so glad! . . . And you think Papa will consent?

ELIZABETH

But of course he will! Both the Doctors are putting it before him as strongly as they can. Oh, surely he'd never have the heart to refuse when he realises all this Italian trip means to me. . . .

ARABEL (without conviction)

No, dear, no. . . .

ELIZABETH

Have you seen him this afternoon?

ARABEL

Yes.

ELIZABETH (quickly)

What was he like?

ARABEL (eagerly)

Oh, quite sunny! He called me "Puss"—and he never does that when he's in one of his moods. And afterwards, when Bella came in, he was really merry.

ELIZABETH

Thank Heaven for that!

ARABEL

Which reminds me, dear—Bella has brought the gown Henrietta is to wear as bridesmaid. They want you to see it. They're trying it on now. . . .

ELIZABETH

Oh, I should love to!

(She pulls the bell-rope.)

I want badly some distraction to help me over the suspense of waiting for Papa's decision. . . .

ARABEL

Somehow I feel, Ba, that it wasn't altogether wise of you to keep this Italian plan secret from Papa, and then spring it suddenly on him.

ELIZABETH

Yes, I know, but—

[A knock at the door.

Come in.

[**WILSON** enters.

Please tell Miss Hedley and Miss Henrietta I shall be delighted to see them now.

WILSON
Yes, Miss.

ELIZABETH
Oh, and take Flush out. He gets so excited when there are several people in the room.

[**WILSON** picks up **FLUSH** and goes out with him.

It was Doctor Chambers himself who advised me to say nothing to Papa until both doctors were satisfied that I was absolutely fit to travel. I quite agreed with him at the time. But now—oh Arabel, I'm not so sure now! I'm so afraid Papa may think—

[Voices and laughter outside.

Don't say anything about this to them. . . .

[**ARABEL** nods.

BELLA (outside)
May we come in?

ELIZABETH (rising)
Come in, dear.

[**BELLA** flutters in followed by **HENRIETTA**, shy but radiant, in her bridesmaid's array.

Bella dear!

BELLA (embracing **ELIZABETH**)
Darling, darling! Oh but you weally shouldn't get up to weceive little me!

ARABEL (contemplating **HENRIETTA**)
How perfectly lovely!

ELIZABETH
Delicious!

BELLA
Yes, isn't it? Isn't she, I should say! Dear Henwietta will be quite the pwettiest of my bwidesmaids. Indeed, I'm afwaid she'll dwaw all eyes from the little bwide! At any wate, all the gentlemen's! . . .But, darling Ba, you weally mustn't stand about like this!

(Leads her to the sofa.)

ELIZABETH
But I'm as well able to stand as anyone nowadays.

BELLA (as **ELIZABETH** submits to be laid on the sofa)
No, no . . . ! One has only to see your dear face, so twansparent and spiwitual, to know how near you are to Heaven. You always have a look in your eyes, darling, as though you alweady saw the angels!

HENRIETTA
She's looking at me, Bella—and I'm no angel!

BELLA
No, I'm afwaid you're not. . . . But you're vewy, vewy beautiful! . . . And fancy, Ba, if I hadn't spoken to Uncle Edward myself, I should never have had her for my bwidesmaid!

ELIZABETH
Yes, my dear, you certainly have a way with you.

HENRIETTA
Spoken to Papa! I like that! Why, you sat on his knee and stroked his whiskers.

ARABEL (reprovingly)
Henrietta dear!

[**ELIZABETH** laughs.

BELLA
And why not. Isn't he my Uncle? . . . Besides that, I think he's most fwightfully thwilling! I adore that stern and gloomy type of gentleman. It's so exciting to coax and manage them. And so easy—if you know how! And I weally think I do. . . . But what I can't understand is his extwaordinawy attitude towards love and ma'wiage, and all that. It isn't as if he were in any way a mis—mis—oh, what's the howwid word?

ELIZABETH
Misogynist?

BELLA
Yes, and—

HENRIETTA
Well, I should describe him as the king of misogynists!

BELLA
But he isn't, I tell you.

HENRIETTA
How do you know?

BELLA
Never mind. But I do know. . . . Besides, didn't he mawwy himself—and, what's more, have eleven childwen? . . .

[An uncomfortable silence.

Oh, have I said anything—vewy dweadful?

ARABEL
No, dear—but, perhaps, not quite nice. When God sends us children it's not for us to enquire how and why. . . .

BELLA
I'm so sowwy! I didn't mean to be i'wevewent. . . . But I do find dear Uncle Edward's attitude extwaordinawy—and so useless! For in spite of it—and wight under his nose—and all unknown to him—his whole house is litewally seething with womance!

ARABEL
Bella!

HENRIETTA (sharply)
What on earth do you mean?

BELLA
You ought to know, darling.

HENRIETTA
I?

BELLA (enthusiastically)
I think Captain Surtees Cook is quite fwightfully thwilling! The way he looks at you, dear—and looks—and looks—and looks! . . . If he ever looked at me like that my knees would twemble so that I shouldn't be able to stand, and I'd get the loveliest shivers down my back!

ARABEL
Really, Bella!

HENRIETTA (vexed and embarrassed)
I've never met anyone who was able to pack more sheer nonsense into a couple of sentences than you.

BELLA
Haven't you, darling? . . . And then, there's George! You may not believe it, but I'm absolutely certain he has a thwilling understanding with your little cousin Lizzie. . . . And you weally mean to tell me that Charles and Miss what's-her-name are just mere fwiends? As for poor Occy—well, I don't mind telling you, in confidence, that my dear, dear Ha'wy is fwightfully jealous of him. . . .

ARABEL
Mr. Bevan jealous of Occy! But why?

BELLA
Why indeed? Aren't gentlemen silly?

ELIZABETH (laughing)
What an extraordinary girl you are, Bella!

BELLA
Oh, I'm a fwightfully observant little thing! F'winstance, though you hardly ever mention his name, I know that Mr. Wobert Bwowning comes here to see you at least once evewy week. And at other times he sends you flowers. And he often bwings little cakes for dear Flush. . . .Flush! Oh, wouldn't it be fwightfully intewesting if only dear Flush could speak!

ARABEL
Good gracious, why?

ELIZABETH (coldly)
But not so interesting as if Bella were occasionally silent.

BELLA
Touché, darling! I know I'm a dweadful little wattle—but you don't weally mind my quizzing you, do you?

ELIZABETH
Not in the least.

BELLA (to **ARABEL**)
You see, dear Flush is the only witness of all that goes on at Ba's weekly tête-à-tête with the handsomest poet in England. He—Flush, I mean—ought to know a wonderful lot about poetwy by this time! For when two poets are gathered together they talk about whymes and whythms all the time? Or don't they? . . . I'm fwightfully ignowant.

ELIZABETH
Oh, no, my dear! On the contrary—you're "fwightfully" knowing.

BELLA
Me?

HENRIETTA
I hope to goodness you won't chatter any of this outrageous nonsense in front of Papa.

BELLA
Nonsense, is it? Well, I've my own little opinion about that! . . . But, of course, I won't bweathe a word of it to Uncle Edward. I'm all on the side of womance, and the path of twue love, and all that. . . .

ARABEL (solemnly)
Bella, I regret to say it, but I think you are one of the few girls I know who would have benefited entirely under Papa's system of upbringing.

[**ELIZABETH**and **HENRIETTA** laugh.

BELLA

Ooh . . . what a thwilling thought! He was always fwightfully stwickt, wasn't he? Did he whip you when you were naughty? How fwightfully exciting to be whipped by Uncle Edward!

[A knock at the door. The **BARRETT** SISTERS are on the alert at once.

ELIZABETH
Come in.

[**BARRETT** enters. **BELLA** jumps to her feet with a little scream and runs up to him.

BELLA
Oh, Uncle Edward!

(She thrusts her hand through his arm and snuggles against him.)

Uncle dear, if I had been your little girl instead of Papa's would you have been te'wibly severe with me? . . . You wouldn't, would you? Or would you?

BARRETT
Would—wouldn't—wouldn't—would? Are you trying to pose me with some silly riddle?

BELLA (drawing him into the room)

No, no, no. Sit down.

(Pushes him into a chair and perches herself on his knee.)

It's like this—But why that gloomy fwown, Uncle Edward? . . .

(She passes her fingers lightly over his forehead.)

There—there—all gone!

[**BARRETT** has slipped his arm round her waist.

Awabel says it would have done me all the good in the world to have been bwought up by you. She thinks I'm a spoilt, fwivolous little baggage, and—

ARABEL
Bella! I never said anything of the sort!

BELLA
I know you didn't. But you do!

(Points to **HENRIETTA** and **ELIZABETH**)

And you do. And you do. . . . But you don't, Uncle, do you?

ARABEL
Really, Bella—

BARRETT (speaking to **BELLA**, but looking at the others)
If my children were as bright and open and affectionate as you are I should be a much happier man.

BELLA
Oh, you mustn't say such things, or they'll hate me . . . !

BARRETT (drawing her close. The two seem to be quite withdrawn from the others and oblivious of them)
And you're a distractingly lovely little creature. . . .

BELLA
Anything w'ong in that?

BARRETT
I didn't say so. . . .

BELLA
Then why do you look at me so fiercely? Do you want to eat me up?

BARRETT
What's that scent you have on you?

BELLA
Scent? Me?

(Giggling and snuggling up to him)

Don't you like it?

BARRETT
I abominate scent as a rule—but yours is different.

BELLA
Nice?

BARRETT
It's very delicate and subtle. . . . Still, I should prefer you not to use it.

BELLA
Why?

BARRETT
Never mind.

(Gently but audibly smacks her thigh.)

BELLA
Ooh—that hurts!

BARRETT
Nonsense.

BELLA (triumphantly)
But I never use scent! I haven't a dwop on me. I think it's ho'wid and common!

(With her arms round his neck)

Oh Uncle, you're a darling! You've called me bwight and open and affectionate, distwactingly lovely and fwagwant all within a few minutes! You may kiss me!

[**BARRETT** kisses her twice so roughly on the mouth that she gives a little cry. Then he pushes her abruptly off his knee and gets to his feet. She looks a little frightened.

BARRETT (brusquely)
There, there, child, run away now. I want to speak to Ba. (To the others) You can go too.

(He crosses to the window and stands looking out, with his back to the room.)

BELLA (in a rather injured voice)
Good-bye, Uncle.

BARRETT (without turning)
Good-bye.

BELLA
Good-bye, Ba.

[With a little toss of her head, she goes out.

ELIZABETH
Good-bye.

[**HENRIETTA** and **ARABEL** go out.

A pause. **ELIZABETH** looks with nervous expectancy at her father, who still stands at the window with his back to the room.

BARRETT (without turning)
When is the wedding?

ELIZABETH
The wedding? Oh, Bella's . . . On the twenty-seventh.

BARRETT (turning, and speaking half to himself)
Good. Less than a fortnight. . . . We are not likely to see much of her till then. And afterwards—well, she'll be living in the country most of the year.

ELIZABETH
But I thought you were so fond of her, Papa.

BARRETT (sharply)
Fond of her? Why not? Isn't she my niece? . . . But she's a disturbing influence in the house. To see your brothers following her about with their eyes—especially Octavius. . . . Faugh! the room is still full of her! I shall be glad when she's gone. . . . But I don't want to talk about Bella. Your doctors have just left me.

ELIZABETH (expectantly)
Yes, Papa . . . ?

BARRETT (with forced heartiness)
Their report is excellent. Astonishing. I'm more than gratified. I'm delighted. . . . Of course, my poor child, it's unlikely that you will ever be a normal woman. Even Chambers—optimistic fool though he is— was forced to admit that. . . . By the way, who is this Doctor Ford-Waterlow?

ELIZABETH
I've been told he is one of the cleverest physicians in London.

BARRETT
Really? . . . Well, he needs some amazing qualities to counterbalance his execrable manners. But even this medical phenomenon is unable to account for the sudden improvement in your health. Puts it down to Chambers' ministrations—which is, of course, arrant nonsense.

ELIZABETH
Perhaps the wonderful weather we've been having has most to do with it. I always thrive in warmth and sunshine.

BARRETT
Rubbish. Last summer was sweltering, and you have never been worse than then. No, to my mind, there is only One whom we have to thank—though this Doctor what's-his-name was pleased to sneer when I mentioned—Him.

ELIZABETH
Him?

BARRETT
I mean Almighty God. . . . It amazes me, Elizabeth, that you, on whom this miracle of recovery has been worked, should ascribe it to mere earthly agencies. Haven't I knelt here night after night and implored our all-loving Father to have compassion on His child? . . . It amazes me. It grieves me unspeakably. That is all I have to say for the present.

(He turns to the door.)

ELIZABETH
Papa.

BARRETT
Well?

ELIZABETH
Didn't Doctor Ford-Waterlow speak to you about—about next winter?

BARRETT
Doctor Ford-Waterlow talked, if I may say so, a great deal of nonsense.

(He turns to go.)

ELIZABETH
But Papa—

BARRETT (testily)
What is it?

ELIZABETH
Didn't he tell you that I should avoid spending next winter in England?

BARRETT
Well?

ELIZABETH
And that he thinks I shall be fit to travel to Italy in October, if you—

BARRETT
So! It's out at last! And how long has this precious plot been hatching, may I ask?

ELIZABETH
It's now several weeks since Doctor Chambers first mentioned Italy as a real possibility.

BARRETT
I see. And do your brothers and sisters know anything of this delightful project?

ELIZABETH
I believe I mentioned it to them.

BARRETT
You believe you mentioned it to them. And Mr. Kenyon, and Mr. Horne, and the Hedleys, and that charlatan Browning—all your friends and relations in short—you've discussed your plans with the lot of them, I suppose?

ELIZABETH
Oh, Papa, what does it matter? My only reason—

BARRETT
Matter? Not in the least! It's nothing at all that I alone should be shut out of my favourite daughter's confidence—treated like a cipher—ignored—insulted—

ELIZABETH
Insulted?

BARRETT
Grossly insulted. When that fellow, Ford-Waterlow, sprung your carefully prepared mine on me and I naturally expressed my astonishment and displeasure, he became extremely offensive, and—

ELIZABETH
Believe me, Papa, my one reason for not worrying you with this Italian idea before was—

BARRETT
The fear that I should nip it in the bud at once. Exactly. I quite understand.

ELIZABETH
But—

BARRETT
No. I beg you to spare me explanations and excuses. The whole miserable business is abundantly clear. I am cut to the heart that you—the only one of my children whom I trusted implicitly—should be capable of such underhand conduct.

ELIZABETH
No—no—

BARRETT
If returning health must bring with it such sad change of character I shall be driven to wish that you were once more lying helpless on that sofa. There is nothing more to be said.

(He turns to the door.)

ELIZABETH (with restrained anger)
But there is more to be said, and I must beg you to listen to me, Papa. How many years have I lain here? Five? Six? It's hard to remember—as each year has been like ten. And all that time I've had nothing to look forward to, or hope for, but death.

BARRETT
Death . . . ?

ELIZABETH
Yes, death. I was born with a large capacity for happiness—you remember me as a young girl?—and when life brought me little happiness and much pain, I was often impatient for the end, and—

BARRETT (outraged)

Elizabeth! I'm shocked that—

ELIZABETH (swiftly)
And now this miracle has happened! Day by day I am better able to take and enjoy such good things as everyone has a right to—able to meet my friends, to breathe the open air and feel the sun, and see grass and flowers growing under the sky. . . . When Doctor Chambers first spoke to me of Italy I put the idea from me—it seemed too impossibly wonderful! But as I grew stronger, it came over me, like a revelation, that Italy wasn't an impossibility at all, that nothing really stood in the way of my going, that I had every right to go—

BARRETT
Right?

ELIZABETH
Yes! every right—if only I could get your consent. So I set about consulting my friends, meeting all obstacles, settling every detail, so as to have a perfectly arranged plan to put before you after the Doctors had given you their opinion. In my eagerness I may have acted stupidly, mistakenly, tactlessly. But to call my conduct underhand and deceitful is more than unkind. It's unjust. It's cruel.

BARRETT (more in sorrow than in anger)
Self! Self! Self! No thought, no consideration, for anyone but yourself, or for anything but your pleasure.

ELIZABETH (passionately)
But Papa—

BARRETT (with a silencing gesture)
Didn't it even once occur to you that all through those long, dark months you proposed to enjoy yourself in Italy, your father would be left here utterly alone?

ELIZABETH
Alone?

BARRETT
Utterly alone. . . . Your brothers and sisters might as well be shadows for all the companionship they afford me. And you—oh, my child, don't think that I haven't noticed that you, too, now that you are stronger and no longer wholly dependent on me, are slowly drawing away from your father. . . .

ELIZABETH
It's not true!

BARRETT
It is true—and, in your heart, you know it's true.

ELIZABETH
No!

BARRETT

New life, new interests, new pleasures, new friends—and, little by little, I am being pushed into the background—I who used to be your whole world, I who love you—who love you—

ELIZABETH
But Papa—

BARRETT (with a silencing gesture)
No. There is nothing more to be said.

(He crosses to the window, looks out, then turns.)

You want my consent for this—Italian jaunt. I shall neither give it nor withhold it. To give it would be against my conscience as encouraging selfishness and self-indulgence. To withhold it would be a futile gesture. You are your own mistress. Even if I refused to pay your expenses, you have ample means of your own to carry out your intentions. You are at liberty to do as you wish. . . . And if you go, I hope you will sometimes spare a thought for your father. Think of him at night stealing into this room which once held all he loved. Think of him kneeling alone by the empty sofa and imploring the Good Shepherd to—

[A knock at the door.

Eh . . . ?

ELIZABETH (with a start, her hand going to her heart)
Oh. . . .

BARRETT (testily)
Who's that? Come in.

[**WILSON** enters.

WILSON
If you please, Mr. Browning has called.

BARRETT (under his breath)
That fellow again . . .

WILSON
I showed Mr. Browning into the drawing-room, Miss, seeing as you were engaged.

ELIZABETH
Would you like to meet Mr. Browning, Papa?

BARRETT
Certainly not. I should have thought you knew by this time that I never inflict myself on any of my children's friends. (To **WILSON**) You may show Mr. Browning up.

WILSON
Very good, sir.

[She goes out.

BARRETT
Mr. Browning appears to consider this his second home.

ELIZABETH
I have not seen him since last Wednesday.

BARRETT
Indeed.

[He goes out.

ELIZABETH sits quite still, breathing quickly, her eyes fixed on the door. **WILSON** enters.

WILSON
Mr. Browning.

[**BROWNING** enters and **ELIZABETH** rises to receive him. **WILSON** goes out.

BROWNING (taking both her hands)
Oh, but how splendid! This is the fourth time you've received me—standing!

ELIZABETH (her whole manner has changed: she is all sparkle and life)
If ever I receive you from my sofa again you may put it down to my bad manners and nothing else!

BROWNING
I will, with all my heart, I will! And now, tell me quickly. I've been dithering with suspense all day. You've seen them? What do they say?

ELIZABETH
Doctor Ford-Waterlow was quite taken out of his grumpy self with astonished delight at my improvement.

BROWNING (delightedly)
Say that again!

ELIZABETH
Oh, must I? The whole sentence?

BROWNING
I should like to see it in letters of fire burning at me from each of these four walls! This is the best moment I've had since I got your note giving me permission to call on you! How many years ago was that?

ELIZABETH
Three months.

BROWNING

Absurd! We've always been friends. I've known you a lifetime and over! So, he was quite taken out of his grumpy self with astonished delight, was he? Splendid! Of course, I never once doubted that you would turn the corner some day. The world isn't rich enough to afford the waste of such a life as yours! But even I little dreamt recovery would be so rapid. And Italy? Are both Doctors agreed about your wintering there?

ELIZABETH (with a note of reserve in her voice)

Yes.

BROWNING

And when do they think you'll be fit for travelling?

ELIZABETH

The middle of October—unless there's a relapse.

BROWNING

Relapse? There isn't such a word! October! Extraordinary! For you know, October suits my own plans to perfection.

ELIZABETH

Your plans?

BROWNING

Don't you remember my telling you that I had thought of wintering in Italy myself? Well, now I am quite decided. You see, I have practically made up my mind to remodel "Sordello." I should never be able to grapple with the task satisfactorily in England. Impossible to get the Italian atmosphere in a land of drizzle and fog! May I call on you often in Italy? Where do you intend to stay?

[**ELIZABETH** laughs.

Why are you laughing?

ELIZABETH

In Italy I'm afraid you'll need seven-league boots—when you call on me!

BROWNING

What do you mean?

ELIZABETH

I shall be at 50, Wimpole Street next winter.

BROWNING

Here?

ELIZABETH

Yes.

BROWNING
But didn't you tell me that both doctors—

ELIZABETH
Doctors may propose; but the decision rests—elsewhere.

BROWNING
Your father?

ELIZABETH
Yes.

BROWNING
He—he has vetoed the plan?

ELIZABETH
No—not exactly. But I am quite sure that he—that it will be impossible for me to go.

BROWNING
But—didn't the doctors make it clear to him that this move of yours may mean all the difference between—life and death?

ELIZABETH
I believe Doctor Ford-Waterlow spoke very forcibly.

BROWNING
Then, in Heaven's name—

ELIZABETH (quickly, nervously)
Oh, it's rather hard to explain to someone who doesn't know all the circumstances. . . . You see, Papa is very devoted to me, and—

BROWNING
Devoted? . . .

ELIZABETH
Very devoted to me—and depends a lot on my companionship. He hasn't many points of contact with my brothers and sisters. If I were away for six months, he—

BROWNING (visibly and audibly putting restraint himself)
Miss Barrett—may I speak plainly?

ELIZABETH (nervously)
Oh, do you think you'd better? I know—more or less—how you feel about this. But you don't quite understand the situation. How should you?

BROWNING

Very well. Then I'll say nothing. . . .

(His control suddenly gives way: his words pour out in a furious torrent.)

You tell me I don't understand. You are quite right. I don't. You tell me he is devoted to you. I don't understand a devotion that demands favours as if they were rights, demands duty and respect and obedience and love, demands all and takes all, and gives nothing in return—I don't understand a devotion that spends itself in petty tyrannies and gross bullying—I don't understand a devotion that grudges you any ray of light and glimpse of happiness, and doesn't even stop at risking your life to gratify its colossal selfishness! Devotion! Give me good, sound, honest hatred rather than devotion like that!

ELIZABETH
Mr. Browning—I must ask you—

BROWNING
Forgive me—but I won't be silent any longer! Even before I met you, I knew that sickness wasn't the only shadow on your life. And all these months—though you never once breathed a syllable of complaint—I felt that other shadow deepening, and I've stood by, and looked on, and said nothing. Who was I to step in between you and the man nature, as an ugly jest, chose for your father? A mere friend! I might find you tired and sick after hateful scenes I could picture only too vividly—and I must pretend to know nothing, see nothing, feel nothing. Well! I've done with pretence from to-day on! I refuse any longer to let myself be gagged and handcuffed! It's not just your comfort and happiness which are at stake now. It's your very life. And I forbid you to play with your life. And I have the right to forbid you.

ELIZABETH (desperately)
No—no—no . . . Oh, please don't say any more!

BROWNING (with compelling ardour)
The right. And you won't deny it—you're too utterly candid and true. At our first meeting you forbade me to speak of love—there was to be nothing more than friendship between us. I obeyed you. But I knew well enough—we both knew—that I was to be much more than just your friend. Even before I passed that door, and our eyes first met across the room, I loved you—and I've gone on loving you—and I love you now more than words can tell—and I shall love you to the end, and beyond. You know that? You've always known?

ELIZABETH (brokenly)
Yes—yes—I've always known. . . . And now for pity's sake—for pity's sake—leave me.

BROWNING (seizing both her hands)
No.

ELIZABETH
Oh please . . . please . . . let me go. Leave me. We must never see each other again.

BROWNING
I shall never let you go. I shall never leave you.

(He draws her into his arms.)

Elizabeth . . . Elizabeth . . .

ELIZABETH (struggling feebly in his embrace)
No—no. . . . Oh Robert, have mercy on me. . . .

BROWNING
Elizabeth, my darling. . . .

(He kisses her; and at the touch of his lips, her arms go round his neck.)

ELIZABETH
Oh Robert, I love you—I love you—I love you. . . .

[They kiss each other again. Then she sinks into a chair, and he kneels beside her holding her hands.

BROWNING
And yet you ask me to take my marching orders and go out of your life?

ELIZABETH
Yes, Robert, for what have I to give you? I have so little of all that love asks for. I have no beauty, and no health, and I'm no longer young. . . .

BROWNING
I love you.

ELIZABETH (with restrained spiritual passion)
I should have refused to see you again after our first meeting. For I loved you then, though I would have denied it—even to myself. . . . Oh, Robert, I think Eve must have felt as I did when her first dawn broke over Paradise—the terror, the wonder, the glory of it! I had no strength to put up any kind of resistance except the pitiful pretence of mere friendship. I was helpless, I was paralysed, with happiness I had never dreamt it was possible to feel. . . . That's my only excuse—and God knows I need one!—for not having sent you away from me at once.

BROWNING
I love you.

ELIZABETH
My life had reached its lowest ebb. I was worn out, and hope was dead. Then you came. . . . Robert, do you know what you have done for me? I could have laughed when Doctor Chambers said that I had healed myself by wanting to live. He was right! oh, he was right! But he little knew what lay behind his words! I wanted to live—eagerly, desperately, passionately—and only because life meant you—you— and the sight of your face, and the sound of your voice, and the touch of your hand. Oh, and so much more than that! Because of you the air once more was sweet to breathe, and all the world was good and green again.

BROWNING (kissing her hands)

And with those words singing in my ears, I'm to turn my back on you and go?

ELIZABETH
But, Robert, can't you—can't you see how impossible—

BROWNING
I've never yet turned my back on a friend or an enemy. Am I likely to turn it on you?

ELIZABETH
But how is it all to end? What have we to look forward to? And how—

BROWNING
I love you—and I want you for my wife.

ELIZABETH
Robert, I can't marry you. How can I when—

BROWNING
Not to-day or to-morrow. Not this year, perhaps, or next. Perhaps not for years to come—

ELIZABETH
I may never be able to marry you.

BROWNING
What then? If you remain to the last beyond my reach, I shall die proud and happy in having spent a lifetime fighting to gain the richest prize a man was ever offered.

ELIZABETH
No—no! Oh, Robert, put aside your dream of me—and look on me as I am. I love you too well to let you waste your manhood pursuing the pale ghost of a woman.

BROWNING
Do you think I'm a boy to be swept off my feet by an impulse? or a sentimental dreamer blind to reality? There's no man alive who sees things as they are with clearer eyes than I do, and has his feet more firmly planted on the earth. And I tell you, in all soberness, that my need of you is as urgent as your need of me. If your weakness asks my strength for support, my abundant strength cries out for your weakness to complete my life and myself.

ELIZABETH (after a pause)
Robert, have you thought what your position here would be like if you went on seeing me after to-day?

BROWNING
Yes.

ELIZABETH (quickly)
We should have to keep our love secret from everyone lest a whisper of it get to my father's ears.

BROWNING

I know.

ELIZABETH
If he had the least suspicion that you were more than a friend, the door would be slammed in your face, my letters supervised, and my life made unbearable.

BROWNING
I know.

ELIZABETH
And you, my dear—you're as frank and open as the day—how would you enjoy coming here under false pretences, and all the deceits, subterfuges, intrigues we'd be forced to use?

BROWNING (with an exultant laugh)
I shall detest it—I shall hate it with all my heart and soul. And I thank God for that!

ELIZABETH
But Robert—

BROWNING
For it's splendid and right that I should suffer some discomfort, at least, for such a reward as you! The immortal garland was never run for without dust and heat!

ELIZABETH (bitterly)
Immortal! Oh Robert, fading, if not already faded!

(He is about to protest.)

No, don't speak! don't speak! . . .

(She rises and goes to the window and looks, with unseeing eyes, into the street. After a moment she turns to him.)

Robert, if we were to say good-bye to-day, we should have nothing but beautiful memories of each other to last to the end of our lives. We should be unhappy; but there are many kinds of unhappiness. Ours would be the unhappiness of those who have put love away from them for the sake of love. There would be no disillusion in it, or bitterness, or remorse.

BROWNING (in a low, tense voice)
Is it you who are speaking?

ELIZABETH
What do you mean?

BROWNING
I don't know you. I thought yours was the courage that dared the uttermost, careless of defeat. Here's life—life—offering us the best that life can give, and you dare not grasp at it for fear it will turn to dust

in your hand! We're to dream away the rest of our lives in tepid sadness rather than risk utter disaster for utter happiness. I don't know you. I never thought you were a coward!

ELIZABETH (proudly, indignantly)

A coward? I?

(With a sudden change of voice)

Yes, I'm a coward, Robert—a coward through and through. . . . But it's not for myself that I'm afraid. . . .

BROWNING (going swiftly up to her and taking her in his arms)
I know that, my darling.

ELIZABETH
What's another disaster, great or small, to me who have known little but disaster all my life? But you're a fighter—and you were born for victory and triumph. If disaster came to you through me—

BROWNING
Yes, a fighter. But I'm sick of fighting alone. I need a comrade-at-arms to fight beside me—and—

ELIZABETH
Not one already wounded in the battle. . . .

BROWNING
Wounded—but undefeated, undaunted, unbroken. . . .

ELIZABETH
Yes, but—

BROWNING
What finer comrade could a man ask for?

ELIZABETH
But Robert—

BROWNING
No.

ELIZABETH
But Robert—

BROWNING
No.

(And he kisses the protest from her lips as the Scene closes.)

ACT IV

HENRIETTA

Some weeks later.

[**ARABEL** enters carrying **FLUSH**. She is in outdoor clothes and has her bonnet on.

ARABEL (standing in the open doorway and speaking)
You had really better let Wilson help you up the last few stairs, Ba.

ELIZABETH (outside)
No! No, Wilson, don't touch me!

ARABEL
But, my dear . . .

[**ELIZABETH** enters, bonneted and in outdoor clothes. She is breathless but triumphant. **WILSON** follows at her heels.

ELIZABETH
There! All the way up, and without one pause or help of any kind! And I feel splendid—just a little out of breath, that's all. . . .

(She sways a little on her feet. Both **WILSON** and **ARABEL** stretch out hands to support her.)

No, don't touch me! I'm perfectly all right. . . .

(She walks to the sofa and sits down, and takes her bonnet and gloves off during the following)

Now wasn't that a glorious triumph? And you know, Wilson, I got out of the carriage and walked quite—two miles in the Park!

WILSON
Lor', Miss!

ARABEL
Ba dear . . . !

ELIZABETH
Well, one mile then. Anyhow, that's what I'm going to tell Doctor Chambers.

ARABEL
Really, Ba . . . !

ELIZABETH

Oh, my dear, Flush has muddied your gown disgracefully! What a filthy state you're in, Flushy! . . . You had better take him, Wilson, and get Jenny to bath him. He's not been properly washed for ages.

WILSON (taking **FLUSH** from **ARABEL**)
Very good, Miss Ba.

[**WILSON** goes out carrying **FLUSH**.

ELIZABETH (pointing to a little heap of letters)
Oh, the post has come. Please give me those letters, dear.

ARABEL (handing her the letters)
Why, that's Mr. Browning's hand-writing! I'm sorry, I couldn't help seeing it, Ba. But aren't you expecting him this afternoon?

ELIZABETH (absently)
Yes. . . .

(she tears open the letter and reads it, smiling to herself)

Yes, dear, he should be here very soon now. . . . This was just to wish me good-night.

ARABEL
To wish you good-night . . . ?

ELIZABETH
Yes, it was written yesterday evening.

ARABEL
Oh. . . .

ELIZABETH (turning over the letters)
Mr. Haydon—Miss Martineau—Mr. Horne—Oh! . . .

(A sharp change coming into her voice.)

This is from Papa.

ARABEL (anxiously)
From Papa! But he's returning to-day. . . .

ELIZABETH
Perhaps he's been detained. . . .

(She opens the letter.)

ARABEL (hopefully)
Oh, do you think so?

ELIZABETH
(she quickly scans the letter; then in a voice of consternation)
Oh! . . . Oh Arabel! . . .

ARABEL
What is it, dear?

ELIZABETH
We're leaving.

ARABEL
Leaving?

ELIZABETH
Yes—leaving this house. Leaving London. Listen—

[A knock at the door and **HENRIETTA**'S voice.

HENRIETTA (outside)
May I come in, Ba?

ELIZABETH
Come in, dear. (In a hurried whisper to **ARABEL**) Don't speak of this yet. . . .

[**HENRIETTA** enters.

HENRIETTA (in great excitement)
Oh, Ba, you must see him at once! You positively must!

ELIZABETH
Him . . . ?

HENRIETTA
He's in his full regimentals. He's just been to St. James's to receive—or whatever you call it—his adjutancy—or something—from Queen Victoria herself. He's wonderful! He's gorgeous! May I bring him up here for you to look at?

ELIZABETH
But—

HENRIETTA
Papa need never know. Oh, Ba, do let me! You've never seen him yet—it's high time you met—and you couldn't see him to better advantage than now! . . . I'm talking of Captain Cook, you know.

ELIZABETH
Yes, so I've gathered. But I can't see him now, dear. I'm expecting Mr. Browning any minute.

HENRIETTA (crestfallen but resigned)
Oh . . . then of course it's impossible. . . . But I tell you what, Ba! I'll try to keep him until Mr. Browning goes. I don't think he'll mind.

(She hurries to the door, and throws over her shoulder)

You can keep your poet here as long as you like.

[She goes out.

ELIZABETH (with a short laugh that ends in a sigh)
Yes, she had best make the most of her soldier while she can, poor darling. She is not likely to see much of him in the future.

(She takes up **BARRETT**'S letter.)

ARABEL
Oh, Ba, tell me quickly. . . .

ELIZABETH
He writes from Dorking. (She reads) "This is to let you know that we shall be leaving London on Monday, the 22nd of this month. I have taken a furnished house at Bookham, in Surrey, some twenty miles from London and six miles from Leatherhead, the nearest railway station. Whether we shall eventually make it our permanent home I have not yet decided. At any rate, we shall spend the winter there. You will benefit by the country air and the complete seclusion of your new surroundings. I have felt for some time now that your present feverishly restless mode of life in London will, if continued, affect you harmfully both physically and morally. I am writing this letter so that you may inform your brothers and sisters of my decision and tell them that I decline absolutely to discuss it when I return home to-morrow."—That's to-day.—"The matter is finally settled, and you and they will make such preparations as are needful for the move."

ARABEL
Oh, Ba! . . .

ELIZABETH (bitterly)
That's not quite all. He finishes up with a characteristic touch of humour.

ARABEL
Humour?

ELIZABETH
Yes. He signs himself—"Your loving Papa."

ARABEL
The twenty-second. That gives us barely a fortnight longer here.

ELIZABETH (stormily)

My "feverishly restless mode of life"!—a few drives, a few calls on my friends, a few visitors. . . . I wonder he doesn't describe me as a recklessly dissipated woman! He made my going to Italy impossible. And now I am to be cut off any little pleasures I have begun to find here.

(She crumples up the letter and tosses it into the grate.)

ARABEL
I know, dear, I understand—and I'm very sorry for you. . . . The change won't hit me so hardly. My only ties in London are my Mission work and district visiting. But you and Henrietta—

(She hesitates.)

ELIZABETH
Well?

ARABEL (with sudden earnestness)
Oh, Ba, don't be angry with me if I tell you that this move may in the long run, be a blessing in disguise for you.

ELIZABETH
A blessing in disguise! I seem to have been brought up on that pious cliché! What do you mean?

ARABEL
We all pretend to be ignorant of each others affairs in this house—except poor Henrietta's. It's safer so. And yet we know—we all know—that you and Mr. Browning—

ELIZABETH
Well?

ARABEL
Oh, Ba, one has only to look at your face when you're expecting him—and again after he has left you. . .
.

ELIZABETH (proudly)
I love him and he loves me. What of it? Haven't I as much right to love and be loved as any other woman?

ARABEL
Oh yes, dear—but how is it all to end? So long as Papa's alive none of us will ever be able to marry with his consent—and to marry without it is unthinkable. And, in your case, it isn't only a question of Papa's consent. . . . Of course it's—it's wonderful how much stronger and better you are—you walked upstairs splendidly just now. . . . But—but—

ELIZABETH
But even if I can manage to walk up a few steps it doesn't mean that I shall ever be fit to marry—is that what you're trying to say?

ARABEL

Oh Ba darling, it's because I love you so dearly, and don't want you to suffer, that I'm forcing myself to speak. I know very little about gentlemen—except that they all want to marry the ladies they fall in love with. I—I don't know Mr. Browning at all—but—But even great poets want to settle down in time, and have a home of their own, and a wife, and—and little ones. . . . It would be so dreadful if—

ELIZABETH (springing to her feet)
Oh, be quiet! be quiet! Do you suppose I haven't thought of all that a thousand times already?

(She goes to the window and looks out.)

ARABEL
I am sorry. . . . I—I didn't mean to interfere. All I want is to save you any—

(She notices that **ELIZABETH** is no longer listening, but is waving her hand to someone in the street, her face transformed with joy.)

Oh . . .

[She rises and slips softly out of the room, unnoticed by **ELIZABETH**.

ELIZABETH (turning)
Mr. Browning has just—

(Realises the empty room)

Oh. . . .

[Her eyes light on **BARRETT**'S crumpled letter in the grate. She picks it up and smooths it out, her face emptied of joy. She puts it on the mantelpiece. A knock at the door.

Come in.

[**BROWNING** enters. They look at each other in silence for a moment; then he goes up to her and takes her in his arms.

BROWNING
My love.

ELIZABETH
Robert. . . .

[They kiss.

BROWNING (holding her at arm's length)
You look tired, sweetheart. What have you been doing to-day?

ELIZABETH (with forced lightness)
I went for a drive—and a walk in the Park. And afterwards I ran all the way upstairs—without help, and

without one stop.

BROWNING
Oh, but you know—! Of course, dearest, it's a splendid feat, and I'm proud of you! . . . Come and sit down.

(Leads her to the sofa, and they sit down.)

Now, aren't you being a trifle too ambitious?

ELIZABETH
I don't think so. . . . I'm feeling wonderfully well. . . .

BROWNING
Look at me.

[She looks at him.

What's the matter, Ba?

ELIZABETH
Nothing. . . .

BROWNING
Has your father returned?

ELIZABETH
No. We expect him to-day.

BROWNING (taking her face in his hands)
Those talking eyes of yours give you hopelessly away. Something has gone wrong. What is it? You must tell me.

ELIZABETH
Read that letter on the mantelpiece, Robert.

BROWNING (goes to the mantelpiece and takes **BARRETT**'S letter)
From your father?

ELIZABETH
Yes.

[He reads the letter; then looks at her with a strange smile on his face.

Well?

BROWNING (still smiling)
I think, by the look of it, you crumpled up this letter furiously in your little hand—and I'm quite sure you

pitched it into the grate.

ELIZABETH
Yes, I did. But—

BROWNING
Why?

ELIZABETH
Oh, Robert, don't you see what this means to us?

BROWNING
Yes—and perhaps better than you do.

ELIZABETH
Better than I? Oh, you mustn't deceive yourself! You think this move will make little difference to us.
You think you'll be able to ride over from London and see me almost as often as we see each other here.
But you're wrong! you're wrong! You don't know Papa as I do. He's grown jealous of my life here, my
pleasures and my friends—and I'm slowly and surely to be parted from them. I've felt this coming for
some time now. Oh, Robert, it will soon be made impossible for me to see you at all. . . .

BROWNING
This precious letter may mean all that. But it means a great deal more that you haven't as yet been able
to grasp.

ELIZABETH
A great deal more . . . ?

BROWNING
It means that you will be in Italy before the month is out.

ELIZABETH (in a whisper)
Italy . . . ?

BROWNING
Yes—and with me.

ELIZABETH
Robert . . .

BROWNING
It means that we must be married at once.

ELIZABETH (standing up)
Do you know what you're saying?

BROWNING
Yes, I know what I am saying. And I repeat it. We must be married at once.

(He goes up to her.)

My darling, listen to me—

(He is about to take her hands.)

ELIZABETH (starting back)
No! Don't touch me! What you say is madness! . . . I can't marry you—I can never marry you.

BROWNING (with a sudden blaze of passion)
You can, and you shall! You'll marry me if I have to carry you out of this house and up to the altar!

(Controlling himself.)

Do you seriously imagine I'm going to allow myself to be elbowed out of your life now? And just to satisfy the selfish jealousy of a man whom I no longer believe to be sane? You ought to know me better by this time—

ELIZABETH (quickly breaking in)
Oh, Robert, it's not only Papa who stands between us. It's I—it's I . . .

BROWNING
We've gone into that a hundred times already, and—

ELIZABETH
Yes, and now we must go into it once again, and frankly, and for the last time.

BROWNING
But—

ELIZABETH (silencing him with a gesture)
Robert, it's no use deceiving ourselves. However much stronger I may become, I shall always remain an invalid. You tell me that you want me sick or well—and it's wonderful of you to say that, and I know you believe it. . . . But I—Robert, I'm not generous enough—I'm too proud, if you like—to accept what I feel through and through, in spite of anything you say, to be a sacrifice of your life and your manhood. As your wife I should be haunted day and night by thoughts of all the glorious things you would have enjoyed but for me—freedom, ease, adventure, and passionate love I—I could never really satisfy. . . .

BROWNING
No—no—listen—

ELIZABETH (with all her soul in her voice)
Oh Robert, I should be haunted by the ghosts of your unborn children. . . . When I read that letter my world seemed to fall to pieces. . . . But now I thank God that it came while we're still free, and have the strength to shake hands and say good-bye. . . .

(She stretches out her hand.)

BROWNING (with a complete change of manner, ignoring her hand, and speaking in a quiet, matter-of-fact voice)
On the whole I think this will be our best plan of campaign. The family leave here on the—

(he consults the letter)

—on the twenty-second. So we have barely a fortnight to get everything done in. You told me last week that Mr. Hedley had invited your sisters to picnic in Richmond Park next Saturday. So the house will be conveniently empty. We'll meet at Mary-le-Bone Church, and be married quietly some time in the morning. I'll see about a licence at once, and interview the Vicar.

ELIZABETH (who has been staring at him with bewilderment and fear)
Robert—

BROWNING (as before)
It would be madness to leave England on the same day. You'll need all the rest and quiet you can get before the journey. So, directly after we are married, I think you had better return here and take things very easily for a day or two. You'll have six days if we leave on Saturday week. Now—

(He takes a paper out of his pocket.)

ELIZABETH
Oh stop! I can't listen to you!

BROWNING (as before, consulting the paper)
For some time now I've kept careful note of the sailings from Southampton in case of just such an emergency as this. The Packet leaves the Royal Pier on Saturdays at nine o'clock. We must catch the five o'clock express at Vauxhall. It arrives at Southampton at eight.

ELIZABETH
Oh . . .

(She laughs wildly, the laugh changing into sobs.)

[**BROWNING** takes her into his arms and draws her down beside him on the sofa. Her sobs gradually subside. She says brokenly

And—and I always believed Papa was the most overbearing man in the world. . . .

BROWNING (smiling)
And yet you've known me for some time now!

ELIZABETH
But I mustn't give way, Robert—I mustn't—I daren't. . . .

BROWNING

There's one other thing, my darling, of the utmost importance that we must settle at once. You can't possibly travel without a maid. Wilson must have a pretty shrewd idea of our relations. You say she is entirely devoted to you. But do you think she will be willing to come
abroad with us?

ELIZABETH (after a pause, in a low voice)
Robert . . . have you ever thought that my strength may break down on the journey?

BROWNING
Yes.

ELIZABETH
Suppose I were to—to die on your hands?

BROWNING (softly, after a slight pause)
Are you afraid, Ba?

ELIZABETH (proudly, indignantly)
Afraid? I? You know that I am not afraid! You know that I would sooner die with you beside me than live a hundred lives without you. . . . But—but how would you feel if I were to die like that? And what would the world say of you? . . .

BROWNING (quietly)
I should be branded as little better than a murderer. And what I should feel I—I leave you to imagine . . .

ELIZABETH
And yet you ask me to come with you?

BROWNING
Yes. I am prepared to risk your life—and much more than mine—to get you out of this dreadful house into the sunshine, and to have you for my wife.

ELIZABETH
You love me like that?

BROWNING
I love you like that.

[A long pause.

ELIZABETH
Robert . . . will you—will you give me a little time?

BROWNING
Time is short, my dear.

ELIZABETH

Yes, I know. But I must have a little time. I can't decide now. I daren't. . . . I feel something must happen soon to show me definitely the way. . . . Give me a few hours. Before I sleep to-night I'll write and tell you my decision. . . . Please, Robert.

BROWNING
You promise me that?

ELIZABETH
I promise.

BROWNING
Very well. . . .

ELIZABETH
Thank you.

BROWNING
Shall I go now?

ELIZABETH
Please. . . .

[He kneels and takes both her hands and presses them passionately to his lips. She receives the caress passively. He rises, and leaves the room in silence.

She sits motionless staring before her. A pause. Then a light knock at the door. Another pause. Then a louder knock. **ELIZABETH** starts out of her thoughts.

Come in.

[**HENRIETTA** enters.

HENRIETTA
I saw Mr. Browning going down the stairs. . . . May I bring him in?

ELIZABETH
Him?

HENRIETTA
He's standing on the landing outside. . . .

(She gives **ELIZABETH** a little shake)

Wake up, Ba! I'm talking of Surtees.

ELIZABETH
Oh yes, of course. . . . But won't some other time do as well?

HENRIETTA

No! No! I told you he was in uniform. You promised to see him, Ba!

ELIZABETH (with a sigh)
Very well, dear. . . .

[**HENRIETTA** kisses **ELIZABETH** impulsively; then goes to the door and opens it.

HENRIETTA (speaking into the passage)
Come in, Surtees.

[**CAPTAIN SURTEES COOK** enters: a huge, handsome, whiskered, frank-faced man. He is arrayed in the full splendour of his "regimentals" and carries his headgear under his arm.

Captain Surtees Cook, Ba.—My sister, Elizabeth.

[**ELIZABETH** has risen to receive him. **COOK** clicks his heels together and bows stiffly.

COOK
Your servant, Miss Barrett.

ELIZABETH   (offering him her hand)
How-do-you-do?

COOK (taking her hand and bowing over it)
Greatly honoured, 'pon my word I am, Miss Barrett. Understand not everyone received here.

HENRIETTA
No indeed, Surtees! With the exception of the family, very few gentlemen have ever been allowed in Ba's room.

COOK
Twice honoured in one day, y'know. First by Her Majesty; now by you, Miss Barrett. Can't think what I've done to deserve it.

ELIZABETH
Oh, I had forgotten! You've just come from the Palace. I have never seen the Queen. What is she like?

COOK
Very little lady, Ma'am; but royal every inch of her.

HENRIETTA
Surtees, you haven't got your sword on!

COOK
Not etiquette, as I told you, to wear it indoors.

HENRIETTA

Oh bother etiquette! I want Ba to see you in full war-paint. Where did you leave it?

COOK
In the hall.

HENRIETTA
I'll fetch it.

(Runs to the door.)

COOK
No, but really—Miss Barrett doesn't want—

[**HENRIETTA** goes out.

ELIZABETH
But indeed I do, Captain Cook! I don't think I've ever seen an officer in . . . full war-paint before, except at reviews and ceremonies—and that was years ago.

COOK
Indeed?

(After a short pause.)

Er—Miss Barrett . . .

ELIZABETH
Yes?

COOK
Miss Barrett . . .

ELIZABETH (encouragingly)
Yes, Captain Cook?

COOK
I say, Miss Barrett. . . .

ELIZABETH
You want to tell me something about Henrietta?

COOK (eagerly)
Just so, Miss Barrett, just so. Exactly. You know, Miss Barrett—you know—

(He is unable to go on.)

ELIZABETH (very kindly)

Yes, Captain Cook, I know. And though I'm quite powerless to help, believe me, you have my heartfelt sympathy.

(She gives him her hand.)

COOK (taking it in both of his)
Thank you. Thank you. More than I deserve. Thank you, Miss Barrett. Never was such a girl, y'know—Henrietta, I mean. Dunno what I've done to deserve—

[**HENRIETTA** enters with the sword. **ELIZABETH** and **COOK** are still holding hands.

HENRIETTA
Oh yes, I thought he'd seize the opportunity to tell you something while I was out of the room. Did he really manage to get it out?

ELIZABETH (smiling)
Perhaps, not quite. Did you, Captain Cook?

COOK
Well—ah—y'know . . . Still, like most ladies—quick in the uptake. . . .

ELIZABETH
Yes, I understood.

(Kissing **HENRIETTA**.)

My dear, how I wish I could do something for you both!

HENRIETTA
Well, you can't, favourite daughter though you are! Nobody can.

(She sits down with the sword across her lap.)

Surtees wants to ask Papa for my hand and all that—quite like the conventional suitor. I can't get it into his poor head that such things are simply not possible at 50, Wimpole Street.

ELIZABETH (earnestly)
Oh believe me, Captain Cook, it would be more than useless! You would be peremptorily ordered out of the house—and I don't know what would happen to Henrietta!

COOK
Quite aware that I'm not much of a match, Miss Barrett. Poor man, y'know. Little else than my pay. Still, quite respectable and all that. Decent family and all that. Should be more than willing, if necessary, to throw up soldiering and take to some money-making business, but—

HENRIETTA
And a fine mess you'd make of it, my poor dear!

COOK
Well, I'm not so sure about that. Admit, of course, that soldiering's my special job. Haven't the brain for much else, I'm afraid. Still, you never know what a fella can't do with a prize like Henrietta to reward his efforts. What d'you say, Miss Barrett?

HENRIETTA
Oh Ba, can you make him understand? I can't!

ELIZABETH (very impressively)
Captain Cook, if you were a Prince of Eldorado and came here courting, with a pedigree of lineal descent from some signory in the Moon in one hand, and a ticket of good behaviour from the nearest Independent Chapel in the other—even then, Papa would show you the door! Now do you understand?

COOK
Can't say I do.

HENRIETTA
Well, anyhow, you're not to speak to Papa, and I forbid you to give up soldiering. Now that I've seen you in your glory, do you suppose I should ever take you without your uniform? Get up. I want to buckle on your sword.

COOK
Aw, I say—

(Stands up, smiling rather sheepishly.)

HENRIETTA (getting to work)
Ba thinks poets are the flower of manhood—a certain poet, at any rate. I mean to show her that she's mistaken. . . .

COOK
I say, you've got it wrong. Sword hangs from the left hip y'know.

HENRIETTA
Why?

COOK
Well—

[**BARRETT** enters, and taking in the scene with a look of amazement, his face immediately hardens into a mould of freezing displeasure. Both **GIRLS** stare at him in consternation. **COOK** stands rigid.

ELIZABETH
Papa. . . . You're—you're home earlier than I expected, Papa.

BARRETT
I don't think I have the privilege of this gentleman's acquaintance.

HENRIETTA
Captain Cook, may I introduce my father? Papa—Captain Surtees Cook.

COOK
Your servant, sir.

[**BOTH MEN** bow stiffly.

HENRIETTA (after a short pause)
Captain Cook is a great friend of George and Occy.

BARRETT
Indeed? (To **COOK**) My sons are very rarely at home at this time of the day.

COOK
Fact is—just passing the house—thought I'd look in on the off chance, y'know, sir—finding one of them in and all that. . . .

BARRETT
I see.

ELIZABETH (breaking a pause)
Captain Cook has just come from Buckingham Palace . . . and Henrietta thought I should like to see him in all the splendour of his regimentals.

BARRETT
Indeed.

(Takes out his watch and looks at it.)

COOK
Nothing much to look at, of course—but ladies like a bit of colour, and er—By Jove, must be getting late!

BARRETT (pocketing his watch)
It's nineteen-and-a-half minutes past five.

COOK
By Jove! High time I were moving. . . .

[**BARRETT** pulls the bell-rope twice.

Good-bye, Miss Barrett.

ELIZABETH
Good-bye, Captain Cook.

(She gives him her hand.)

[**BARRETT** crosses to the door and holds it open.

COOK
Good-bye, Miss Henrietta.

HENRIETTA
I'll see you out.

[**COOK** moves to the door followed by **HENRIETTA**.

COOK (to **BARRETT**)
Your servant, sir.

[**BARRETT** returns his bow in silence. **COOK** goes out and **HENRIETTA** is about to follow. **BARRETT** stays
her with a gesture.

HENRIETTA
I am seeing Captain Cook to the door.

BARRETT
The servant will attend to that.

[He closes the door, and, in silence, crosses to the fireplace and takes up his stand in front of it. When he
speaks he looks straight before him.

Your list of gentlemen visitors appears to be lengthening, Elizabeth.

ELIZABETH
This is the first time I have had the pleasure of meeting Captain Cook.

BARRETT
Indeed. But I infer, from what I saw as I came into the room, that Henrietta's acquaintance is of
somewhat longer standing? Or am I mistaken?

HENRIETTA
I have known Captain Cook for some time now.

BARRETT
Ah. And since when has it been your custom to buckle on his accoutrements?

HENRIETTA
I have never seen him in uniform before.

BARRETT
And I think it improbable that you will see him in uniform, or in mufti, very frequently in the future.

HENRIETTA (in a strained voice)
Why?

BARRETT (ignoring the question)

Again I may be mistaken, but I was under the impression, Elizabeth, that notice should be given me before strangers visited you here.

ELIZABETH

One can hardly describe a friend of George and Occy as a stranger, Papa.

HENRIETTA

Is Captain Cook to be forbidden the house because I helped him on with his sword?

BARRETT (to **ELIZABETH** , ignoring **HENRIETTA**)

You received my letter?

ELIZABETH

Yes, Papa.

BARRETT

What has just happened fully confirms me in the wisdom of my decision. This house is fast becoming a rendezvous for half London. I have neither time nor inclination to find out whether all the persons visiting here are desirable acquaintances for my children. Fortunately our new home is so far from town that your London friends are not likely to trouble us—at least, during the winter.

HENRIETTA (blankly)

Our new home? . . .

BARRETT (to **ELIZABETH**)

You have not told your sisters?

ELIZABETH

Arabel knows.

HENRIETTA

I don't understand. Are we—are we leaving Wimpole Street?

BARRETT (without looking at **HENRIETTA**)

I have taken a house at Bookham, in Surrey. And we move in on the twenty-second.

HENRIETTA

Why?

BARRETT

I am not in the habit of accounting for my actions to anyone—least of all, to my children.

HENRIETTA

But one thing I have a right to ask you, Papa. If Captain Cook is to be forbidden to visit us, is it because you found him here in Ba's room and saw me fastening on his sword?

BARRETT (after a slight pause, looking fixedly at her)
I understood you to say that Captain Cook is George's friend and Occy's.

HENRIETTA
Yes . . . and my friend too.

BARRETT
Ah.

HENRIETTA
Yes, and since it was I who suggested his seeing Ba, and I who asked him to show me how to buckle on his sword, it's unjust to penalise him for—

ELIZABETH (warningly)
Henrietta . . .

BARRETT (to **HENRIETTA** in a sharp low voice)
Come here.

HENRIETTA (she takes a few steps towards him and speaks, a little breathlessly)
Yes, Papa . . . ?

BARRETT (looks at her steadily under lowered brows for a moment, then points to the floor at his feet)
Come here.

[She goes right up to him, breathing quickly and fearfully. He keeps his eyes fixed on her face. Then in a low, ominous voice.

What is this fellow to you?

HENRIETTA
I—I've told you. . . . He's a friend of ours.

BARRETT
What is he to you?

HENRIETTA
A—a friend. . . .

BARRETT
Is that all?

HENRIETTA
Yes.

BARRETT (suddenly grasping her wrist, his voice like the crack of a whip)
You liar!

ELIZABETH (sharply)
Papa . . . !

HENRIETTA (gaspingly)
Let me go!

BARRETT (tightening his grip)
What's this man to you? Answer me.

[She tries to free herself and cries out.

Answer me.

HENRIETTA
Oh Papa . . . please . . .

BARRETT
Answer me.

HENRIETTA
Oh don't . . . don't . . .

BARRETT
Answer me.

HENRIETTA (in a strangled voice)
He's—he's—oh, Papa, I love him—

BARRETT
Ah . . .
(Between his teeth, seizing her other wrist and forcing her to her knees)
Ah—you—you—you—

(She gives a cry of pain.)

ELIZABETH (seizing **BARRETT**'S arm)
Let her go, Papa! I won't have it! Let her go at once!

[**BARRETT** flings **HENRIETTA** off. She collapses in a heap on the floor, sobbing, her face buried in her hands.

BARRETT (turning on **ELIZABETH**)
And you—you knew of this—filthiness?

ELIZABETH
I've known for some time that Henrietta loved Captain Cook, and I've given her all my sympathy.

BARRETT

You dare to tell me—

ELIZABETH
Yes. And I would have given her my help as well, if I had had it to give.

BARRETT
I'll deal with you later. (To **HENRIETTA**) Get up.

HENRIETTA (suddenly clasping his knees and speaking in a voice of passionate entreaty)
Oh, Papa, please listen to me—please. I—I'm not a bad girl—I swear to you I'm not. I know I've deceived you—and I'm sorry—I'm sorry. . . . But I couldn't help it. I—I love him—we love each other—and if you'd known you would have turned him from the house. . . . Oh, can't you understand—won't you try to understand? . . . He's poor—we don't expect to be married yet—but he's a good man—and it can't be wrong to love him. Other women love—why must I be forbidden? I want love—I can't live without love. Remember how you loved Mamma and how she loved you—and—and you'll understand and pity me. . .
.

BARRETT (inexorably)
Get up.

HENRIETTA
Have pity on me, Papa. . . .

BARRETT
Get up.

(He forcibly loosens her hold of his knees, and she staggers to her feet.)

Sit there.

(He points to a chair.)

[She drops into it, and sits listlessly with drooped head.

How long has this been going on?

[**HENRIETTA** says nothing.

Do you hear me? How long have you been carrying on with this fellow?

HENRIETTA
I—I've known him a little over a year.

BARRETT
And you've been with him often?

HENRIETTA
Yes.

BARRETT
Alone?

HENRIETTA
Yes.

BARRETT
Where?

HENRIETTA
We—I—I've met him in the Park, and—and—

BARRETT
And—here?

HENRIETTA
Yes.

BARRETT
Here. And alone?

[**HENRIETTA** is silent.

Have you met him in this house alone?

HENRIETTA
Yes.

BARRETT
So! Furtive unchastity under my own roof—and abetted by one whom I believed to be wholly chaste and good. . . .

HENRIETTA
No—no—

ELIZABETH (fiercely)
How dare you, Papa!

BARRETT
Silence! (To **HENRIETTA**, his voice hard and cold as ice) Now attend to me. Something like this happened a year or two ago, and I thought I had crushed the devil in you then. I was wrong. It needed sterner measures than I had the courage to use. . . . So now, unless I have your solemn word that you will neither see nor in any way communicate with this man again, you leave my house at once, as you are, with nothing but the clothes you have on. In which case, you will be your own mistress, and can go to perdition any way you please. But of this you may be certain. Once outside my doors you will never again be admitted, on any pretext whatever, so long as I live. I think by this time you have learnt that it's

not my habit to make idle threats, and that I never go back on my word. Very well. You have your choice. Take it.

HENRIETTA (after an agonised mental struggle)
Is it nothing to you that I—that I shall hate you for this to the end of my life?

BARRETT
Less than nothing.

HENRIETTA
But—but I must let Captain Cook know that—

BARRETT
I will deal with Captain Cook.

HENRIETTA (desperately)
But Papa—

BARRETT
Will you give me your word neither to see nor to communicate with this man again?

HENRIETTA (after a pause, in a dead voice)
I—I have no choice.

BARRETT
Give me your Bible, Elizabeth.

ELIZABETH
Why?

BARRETT
I am not prepared to accept your sister's bare promise. But I think even she would hesitate to break an oath made with her hand resting on the Word of God. Give me your Bible.

ELIZABETH
My Bible belonged to Mamma. I can't have it used for such a purpose.

BARRETT
Give me your Bible.

ELIZABETH
No.

BARRETT
You refuse?

ELIZABETH
Yes.

[**BARRETT** pulls the bell-rope. A pause. No one speaks or moves. **WILSON** enters.

BARRETT
I want you to go to my bedroom and fetch my Bible. Are your hands clean?

WILSON (looking at her hands)
My hands, sir?

BARRETT
Are they clean?

WILSON (with a touch of asperity)
Yes, sir. I've just been helping to bath Flush.

BARRETT
You will find the Bible on the table beside my bed.

WILSON
Very good, sir.

[She goes out. All three are silent and motionless until she returns.

WILSON re-enters with **BARRETT**'S Bible. She gives it to him and goes out.

BARRETT (to **HENRIETTA**, placing the Bible reverently on the table)
Come here.

[**HENRIETTA** rises and goes to the table.

Place your hand upon the Book.

[She does so.

Repeat after me: "I give you my solemn word that I will neither see, nor have any communication with, Captain Cook again."

HENRIETTA (in a toneless voice)
I give you my solemn word that I will neither see, nor have any communication with, Captain Cook again.

BARRETT
You will now go to your room and remain there until you have my permission to leave it.

[Without a word, but with her head held high, **HENRIETTA** goes out.

(After a pause)

Have you anything to say to me, **ELIZABETH**?

ELIZABETH

No.

BARRETT

Then I must leave you under my extreme displeasure. I shall not see you again, I can have nothing to do with you, until God has softened your heart, and you repent of your wickedness, and ask for His forgiveness, and . . . mine.

[He takes his Bible and goes out.

The moment he has closed the door **ELIZABETH** gets up and pulls the bell-rope. She does so with an air of decision. A pause. **WILSON** enters.

ELIZABETH

Shut the door, please. (Impulsively) Wilson, are you my friend?

WILSON (bewildered)

Your . . . friend, Miss?

ELIZABETH

Yes, my friend. I am in dire need of friendship and help at the moment.

WILSON

I—I don't quite understand, Miss Ba. . . . But I'm that fond of you—I'd do anything to help you.

ELIZABETH

You would? And I know I can trust you?

WILSON

Yes, indeed, Miss.

ELIZABETH

Wilson, next Saturday I am going to marry Mr. Browning.

WILSON (with a gasp)

Marry . . . !

ELIZABETH

Hush. . . . Yes. Of course nobody in this house knows—and nobody must know.

WILSON

Lor', Miss, I should just think not indeed!

ELIZABETH

We're to be married secretly at Mary-le-Bone Church. Will you come with me?

WILSON

Me, Miss? Yes, Miss—and gladly . . .

ELIZABETH
Directly afterwards I shall return here for a few days, and—

WILSON (in boundless amazement)
Here! With Mr. Browning . . . !

ELIZABETH (with an hysterical laugh)
No—no—no! Just alone with you. . . . Then, on the following Saturday, I shall join Mr. Browning, and we're going abroad. . . . We're going to Italy. . . . Will you come with us?

WILSON (in a whisper)
To Italy . . . ?

ELIZABETH
Yes. . . . Will you come with me?

WILSON
Well, Miss, I can't see as how I can help myself. Not that I hold with foreign parts—I don't. But husband or no husband, you'd never get to Italy alive without me.

ELIZABETH
Then you'll come? Then you'll come! Oh, I am so glad! I'll tell Mr. Browning—I'm writing to him now. And I shall want you to take the letter to the post at once. Go and put on your things—I'll have finished by the time you're ready.

WILSON
Yes, Miss.

[**WILSON** goes out, and **ELIZABETH** takes pen and paper and starts writing rapidly as the Scene closes.

ACT V

PAPA

SCENE I

ELIZABETH is kneeling beside **FLUSH** and fastening a lead on to his collar. She pats his head abstractedly, rises, and picks up a little heap of letters in their envelopes from the table, runs through them and places them on the mantelpiece. Then, with a shuddering sigh, she walks to the window, clasping and unclasping her hands in agitation. After standing at the window for a moment, she sighs again and returns to the mantelpiece, picks up the letters and replaces them one by one on the table. Her cloak and bonnet and gloves, etc., are on the bed.

WILSON hurries into the room with two travelling rugs on her arm.

WILSON
Oh, Miss Ba, I'm that sorry! In my flurry to get the luggage off to the railway station yesterday I clean forgot to pack these rugs. And there was heaps of room in the carpetbag.

ELIZABETH
Never mind.

WILSON (placing the rugs across the back of a chair)
I do hope we haven't forgotten nothing else.

ELIZABETH
And if we have it won't matter much. Mr. Browning insisted that we should travel as lightly as possible. We shall be able to get all we need in Paris.

WILSON
Lor', Miss, it don't seem possible we'll be in Paris to-morrow!

ELIZABETH
No. . . .

(She consults her watch.)

Oh, how the time crawls! We've still an hour and a half of this dreadful waiting. . . .You're sure, Wilson, they quite understood at the livery stables exactly when, and where, the cab was to meet us?

WILSON
Oh yes, Miss, I was most particular to see that the young man took it all down—the cab to be at the corner of Wimpole Street at ha'-past three punctual. It won't take us more than ten minutes to get to Hodgson's Library—and then Mr. Browning will have us in his charge.

(Her voice drops to a warm confidential tone.)

Your husband, Miss Ba dear . . .

ELIZABETH
Oh hush! hush! Don't breathe that word here. . . .

WILSON
But, Miss Ba—

ELIZABETH
I'm foolishly nervous, but I can't help it. The very walls seem to be listening. There is no one in the house, I know, except Miss Henrietta—and she should have gone out by now. Still—

WILSON
Miss Henrietta was putting on her bonnet as I came along the passage.

ELIZABETH
Oh Wilson, it's impossible to believe that in little more than an hour I shall have left this room, never, in all likelihood, to see it again. . . .

WILSON
And glad you'll be to see the last of it, I'm sure, Miss Ba.

ELIZABETH
Yes—and no. . . . I've been very miserable here, and very happy. . . . Oh, I wish it were time to go! This waiting is killing me!

WILSON
Have you finished writing your letters, Miss?

ELIZABETH (almost hysterically)
Yes. Yes. I've written to them all to tell them what I've done and to wish them good-bye. I've just been reading over my letter to Mr. Barrett to see if there was something I could add—something—anything. But I can't think—I can't think. . . .

WILSON
Least said, soonest mended, Miss. (With a chuckling laugh) Oh, Miss Ba, I know I shouldn't say such things—but there's a lot I'd give to be here to-night when the Master reads your letter and knows you've
been a married lady for almost a week. . . .

ELIZABETH (quickly)
Don't, Wilson, don't! The very thought terrifies me! I can see his face—I can hear his voice. . . . Thank God, we shall be miles and miles away. . . .

(She looks at her watch.)

An hour and twenty minutes still. Will time never pass?

WILSON (after a pause)
Why don't you write some po'try, Miss?

ELIZABETH (dumbfounded)
Poetry . . . ?

WILSON
Yes, Miss. That 'ud make the time pass nicely, I'm sure.

[**ELIZABETH** breaks into rather hysterical laughter. **HENRIETTA** enters in her shawl, and bonnet. She has a letter in her hand. **ELIZABETH** abruptly stops laughing, and looks at her with frightened eyes.

ELIZABETH (hastily turning her letters on to their faces)
I—I thought you had gone out.

HENRIETTA
Wilson, I want to speak to Miss Ba.

WILSON
Yes, Miss.

[She goes out.

HENRIETTA
I was just going when I ran into a messenger at the door. He brought this letter. It's for you.

ELIZABETH (anxiously, reaching out her hand)
For me?

HENRIETTA (retaining the letter)
Yes. But it's in—in his hand-writing.

ELIZABETH
Captain Cook's?

HENRIETTA
Yes.

ELIZABETH
Open it, dear.

HENRIETTA (tears open the letter and reads): "Dear Miss Barrett, I know I am doing very wrong in drawing you once again into my, and Henrietta's, affairs. But the matter is so urgent I am sure you will forgive me. My regiment has been ordered to Somerset at short notice—and I must positively see Henrietta before I go. If I wrote to her direct, my letter would certainly be read by Mr. Barrett. I understand he opens all her correspondence. Hence my trespass on your kindness. Will you please give Henrietta the enclosed letter, and believe me your grateful and obedient servant, Surtees Cook." . . . Somerset . . .

(She drops the letter, opens the enclosure and reads it eagerly. **ELIZABETH** picks up the letter and tears it into little pieces.)

What is the time?

ELIZABETH
A quarter past two.

HENRIETTA (in a low, tense voice)
You remember Papa threatened to turn me out of the house unless I swore on the Bible not to write to or see Surtees?

ELIZABETH
Yes.

HENRIETTA (defiantly)
Well, I'm going to break that "Bible oath" to-day.

ELIZABETH (quietly)
Are you, dear?

HENRIETTA (More defiantly still)
Yes—and I shall glory in breaking it! Surtees says he'll be at—never mind where!—between four and six—the only free time he has—every day until he leaves next Wednesday. We shall all have left here on Monday; so I must meet him either to-day or to-morrow. I shall meet him both days. And if Papa asks me where I have been—I shall go out of my way to lie to him as often and as grossly as I can.

ELIZABETH (quietly)
I see. Why do you tell me all this?

HENRIETTA (belligerently)
Because I want you to say that I'm a wicked, deceitful, perjured, loose woman, so that I can fling the words back in your face!

(Suddenly throws her arms round **ELIZABETH**.)

Oh Ba darling, forgive me! I'm not myself these days. I am all love and hate—and I don't know which is the worse torture. . . .

ELIZABETH (with passionate tenderness)
My dear, my dear, you think I don't understand! Oh, but I do! I do! And I feel for you and pity you with all my heart! . . . I can do nothing to help you. I daren't even advise you. . . . But never lose hope—never lose courage—never—

[**WILSON** flashes into the room. She is in a state of uncontrolled agitation.

WILSON (gaspingly)
Oh, Miss Ba—Miss Ba . . . !

[Both sisters stare at her, **HENRIETTA** astonished, **ELIZABETH** in terror.

ELIZABETH
What is it, Wilson? (To **HENRIETTA**) Shut the door.

WILSON
The Master, Miss! He—he's just come in. . . .

ELIZABETH (in a whisper)
Papa . . .

WILSON
Yes—just this minute. . . . He must 'ave 'eard—someone must have told him—

ELIZABETH
Be quiet.

HENRIETTA (who has been looking in bewilderment from one to the other)
But Ba, what on earth is the matter?

ELIZABETH
Nothing. Nothing. It's—it's only that Papa hasn't been to see me for ten days now—ever since—you
remember—? And—and scenes of forgiveness are always trying. . . . (To **WILSON**, sharply) Put
away my hat and cloak. Quick.

[**WILSON** does so.

HENRIETTA
I don't believe that's all. You're as white as a sheet. What did Wilson mean? Ba, is there anything I can—

ELIZABETH (softly, intensely)
No, no, no! Don't speak—don't ask me anything. . . . You know nothing—you understand?—nothing—
nothing.

HENRIETTA
But—

ELIZABETH
No. (To **WILSON**) Those rugs . . .

[**WILSON** picks them up. There is a knock at the door. **WILSON** gasps. **ELIZABETH** speaks in a whisper.

Come in.

(She clears her throat, then louder)

Come in.

[**BARRETT** enters. They are all standing in tense attitudes. **ELIZABETH** commands her voice.

You're home early, Papa. . . .

[**BARRETT**, without replying, looks at each of the three in turn; then crosses to the fireplace. **WILSON**,
obviously terror-stricken, slips out of the room, the rugs over her arm.

BARRETT (to **ELIZABETH**)
What's the matter with that girl?

ELIZABETH
Wilson?

BARRETT
Yes. . . . And with you?

ELIZABETH
Nothing, Papa. . . .

BARRETT (after staring broodingly at her for a moment, he turns to **HENRIETTA**)
Where have you been?

HENRIETTA
Nowhere.

BARRETT
Where are you going?

HENRIETTA
To tea with Aunt Hedley.

BARRETT
Is that the truth?

HENRIETTA
Yes.

BARRETT
You remember your oath?

HENRIETTA
Yes.

BARRETT
Have you kept it?

HENRIETTA
Yes.

BARRETT
Are you going to keep it?

HENRIETTA
Yes.

BARRETT (after staring at her for a moment)
I want to speak to your sister. You can go.

[Without a glance at either of them, **HENRIETTA** goes out. **ELIZABETH**

sits perfectly still, waiting. **BARRETT** walks to the window; then turns and goes up to her.

Do you know why I am back so early?

ELIZABETH (in a whisper)
No, Papa.

BARRETT (in a low, intense voice)
Because I could bear it no longer.... It's ten days since last I saw you....

ELIZABETH
Am I to blame for that, Papa?

BARRETT (with restrained fury)
You dare to ask me such a question? Weren't you a party in your sister's shameless conduct? Haven't you encouraged her? Haven't you helped her? Haven't you defended her? And did you expect to go scot-free of my displeasure?

(Stopping himself with a violent gesture)

I've not come to speak about that—but to put it behind me—to forget it—to forget it.... I wonder, my child, have you been half so miserable these last ten days as your father?

ELIZABETH
Miserable, Papa?

BARRETT
Do you suppose I'm happy when I'm bitterly estranged from all I love in the world? Do you know that night after night I had to call up all my will-power to hold me from coming here to forgive you?

ELIZABETH
Papa—

BARRETT
All my will-power, I tell you—all my sense of duty and right and justice.... But to-day I could bear it no longer. The want of your face and your voice became a torment. I had to come. I am not so strong as they think me. I had to come. And I despise myself for coming—despise myself—hate myself....

ELIZABETH
No—no!

(Suddenly rises and puts her hands on his shoulders.)

Oh, Papa, can't you see, won't you ever see, that strength may be weakness, and your sense of justice and right and duty all mistaken and wrong?

BARRETT (hoarsely, taking her hands from his shoulders)

Mistaken and wrong? What do you mean? . . .

(Quickly stopping her from speaking)

No, be silent. Don't answer me. . . . Mistaken and wrong? You don't know what you're saying.

ELIZABETH
If you'll only listen to me, Papa, I—

BARRETT
No.

ELIZABETH
But, Papa—

BARRETT
No.

(He moves to the window and stands there, his face half averted from her. A pause. He turns.)

If there were even a vestige of truth in what you say, my whole life would be a hideous mockery. For always—through all misfortunes and miseries—I've been upheld by knowing, beyond a doubt, what was right, and doing it unflinchingly, however bitter the consequences. . . . And bitter they've been—how bitter, only God knows! It's been my heavy cross that those whom I was given to guide and rule have always fought against the right that I knew to be the right—and was in duty bound to impose upon them. . . . Even you. Even your Mother.

ELIZABETH (in a whisper)
My Mother? . . .

BARRETT
Yes, your Mother. . . . But not at first. . . . You—you, my eldest child, were born of love and only love. . . . But the others—long before they came the rift had begun to open between your Mother and me. Not that she ever opposed me—never once. Or put into words what she felt. She was silent and dutiful and obedient. But love died out—and fear took its place—fear. . . .

ELIZABETH (sharply)
No! No!

BARRETT
And all because I saw the right—and did it.

ELIZABETH
(in a low voice, staring before her)
Oh . . . oh dear God, what she must have suffered. . . .

BARRETT
She?—She? . . . And what of me? What of me?

ELIZABETH
You? . . . Oh Papa, then you—you still loved her—after her love for you had died? . . .

BARRETT (in a muffled voice, looking aside)
Love. . . ? What's love? . . . She was my wife. . . . You—you don't understand. . . .

ELIZABETH (in a horrified whisper)
And all those children . . . born in fear. . . . Oh, it's horrible—it's horrible—it's horrible. . . .

(With a shuddering sob, she covers her face with her hands.)

BARRETT (aghast and embarrassed)
Ba, my dear—don't—don't . . . I—I shouldn't have spoken—I shouldn't have told you all that. . . . Forget it, child. . . .

(He goes up to her)

Take your hands from your face. . . .

(He gently touches her wrists.)

[She starts away from him, looking at him with wide, frightened eyes.

Don't look at me like that.

(In a low, thick voice, averting his eyes)

You don't understand. How should you? You know nothing of the brutal tyranny of—passion, and how even the strongest and best are driven by it to Hell. Would you have abetted your sister in her—

ELIZABETH (fiercely)
Henrietta's love—how dare you speak of it in the same breath as—

BARRETT (brutally)
Her love? You ignorant little fool! What do you know of love? Love! The lust of the eye—the lowest urge of the body—

ELIZABETH (springing to her feet)
I won't listen to you!

BARRETT (seizing her wrists and forcing her back to her seat)
You must—you shall! It's time a little reality were brought into your dream of life. Do you suppose I should have guarded my house like a dragon from this so-called love if I hadn't known, from my own life, all it entails of cruelty and loathing and degradation and remorse? . . .

(He pulls himself together.)

With the help of God, and through years of tormenting abstinence, I strangled it in myself. And so long as I have breath in my body, I'll keep it away from those I was given to protect and care for. You understand me?

ELIZABETH (in a low voice, looking him full in the face)
Yes—I understand you . . . I understand you. . . .

BARRETT
Very well.

[A pause. **ELIZABETH** sits quite still looking before her. When he speaks again his voice has changed.

This has been a hateful necessity. I had to speak—plainly—lest your very innocence should smirch the purity I am utterly resolved to maintain in my home. . . . And because I feel that you acted in innocence and ignorance, I—I forgive you freely, my child. . . . We must turn over this ugly page—and forget what was on it. . . .

(He takes her hand.)

You're—cold as ice. . . . Why are you trembling?

ELIZABETH (drawing her hand from his)
I shall never forget what you have said.

BARRETT
Never forget—but—And yet, perhaps that's as well. . . .

(With sudden urgency)

But for God's sake, my darling, don't let this raise any further barrier between us! I've told you how all these past months I've seemed to feel you slipping little by little away from me. . . . Your love is all I have left to me in the world.

ELIZABETH
You had Mamma's love once. You might have had the love of all your children.

BARRETT
Yes, if I'd played the coward's part, and taken the easier way, and shirked my duty. I'd rather be hated by the whole world than gain love like that.

ELIZABETH (in a broken voice)
Oh Papa, you—you don't know how I pity you. . . .

BARRETT (roughly)
Pity? I don't want your pity. . . . But if I should ever lose you or your love—

(He seizes her unwilling hands.)

My darling, next week we shall have left this house, and I hope we shall never return here. I've grown to loathe it. In our new home we shall draw close to each other again. There will be little to distract you in the country—nothing and no one to come between us.

(He draws her stiffening form into his arms.)

My child, my darling, you want me to be happy. The only happiness I shall ever know is all yours to give or take. You must look up to me, and depend on me, and lean on me. You must share your thoughts with me, your hopes, your fears, your prayers. I want all your heart and all your soul. . . .

(He holds her passionately close; she leans away from him, her face drawn with fear and pain.)

ELIZABETH (sobbingly)
I can't bear it—I can't bear any more. . . . Let me go, Papa—please let me go. . . .

[He loosens his embrace, and she falls away from him, her arm covering her face. He rises and bends over her.

BARRETT
Forgive me, dear. I've said too much. I was carried away. I'll leave you now.

ELIZABETH (in a whisper)
Please . . .

BARRETT
Shall I see you again to-night?

ELIZABETH (as before)
Not to-night. . . .

BARRETT
I shall pray for you.

ELIZABETH (half to herself)
Pray for me? . . . To-night. . . .

(She turns and looks up at him.)

Yes, pray for me to-night—if you will. . . .

[He kisses her forehead gently, and goes out. She sits for a moment looking before her, and then, with frightened eyes, round the room. She whispers—

I must go at once—I must go—I must go. . . .

(She gets up quickly, and fetches her cloak and bonnet from the wardrobe.)

[**WILSON** enters, stealthily and hurriedly, the rugs on her arm.

WILSON
He's gone to the study.

ELIZABETH (putting on her bonnet)
We must go. Now. At once.

WILSON
But, Miss Ba—

ELIZABETH
At once. Help me on with my cloak.

WILSON (doing so)
But the cab won't be there yet—not for an hour. Besides—

ELIZABETH
Then we must walk about the streets. I can't stay here any longer. I'm frightened. I'm frightened. Fetch your cloak and bonnet.

WILSON
Walk about the streets, Miss? You can't—you can't. Besides—the Master's at home. He may see us leaving. For God's sake, Miss—-

ELIZABETH
Where did I put those letters? Ah, here. . . .

(Spreading them out on the table)

Fetch your cloak and bonnet. Quick.

WILSON
But if he saw us leaving—

ELIZABETH
We must chance that.

WILSON
But, Miss Ba—

ELIZABETH
He can't stop me. I don't belong to him any more. I belong to my husband. Papa can kill me. But he can't stop me.

WILSON
I daren't, Miss, I daren't.

ELIZABETH

Then I must go alone.

WILSON
You can't do that.

ELIZABETH (with compelling earnestness)
Wilson, things have passed between my father and me which force me to leave this house at once. Until to-day I didn't realise quite how unforgivably I have been driven to deceive him. Until to-day—I've never really known him. He's not like other men. He's—dreadfully different. . . . I—I can't say any more. . . . If you want to draw back you need never reproach yourself. This, after all, is no affair of yours. But I must go now.

WILSON
I'll fetch my cloak and bonnet at once, Miss.

[**ELIZABETH** puts her arm round **WILSON**'S neck and kisses her.

Oh, Miss Ba . . .

[**WILSON** goes out quickly. **ELIZABETH** spreads the letters on the table. Then, from a ribbon on which it is hung, she draws her wedding ring from her bosom. She slips it on to her finger; looks at it for a moment; then pulls on her gloves. **WILSON** re-enters, softly and quickly, in cloak and bonnet.

ELIZABETH
I am quite ready. You take the rugs, Wilson. I had better carry Flush.

WILSON (breathlessly)
Yes, Miss.

ELIZABETH
And now slip downstairs and see whether the study door is shut.

WILSON
Yes, Miss.

[**WILSON** goes out, leaving the door open. **ELIZABETH** picks up **FLUSH**, and stands with him under her arm, and looks round the room with an indescribable expression on her face. **WILSON** re-enters.

WILSON (in a whisper)
The door's shut—and all's quiet.

ELIZABETH
Very well.

[She passes out, and **WILSON** follows, closing the door softly after her.

For a moment the room stands empty. Then the Scene slowly closes.

SCENE II

The curtain rises on the still empty room. An hour or two has elapsed. The sky, seen through the window, is full of colour from the after-glow. A pause. **ARABEL** enters.

ARABEL (on entering)
Ba dear, I want—

(She realises the room's emptiness and stares bewildered around her. Her eyes light on the letters Elizabeth has left. Leaving the door open, she goes to the table and looks at them. She picks up a letter, and whispers, visibly agitated)

For me. . . . What can it mean . . . ?

(She tears open the letter, and reads it with little gasping exclamations) Oh . . . ! No, no . . . ! Married . . . ! No . . . ! Oh . . . Oh . . . !

(She looks up from the letter, her face transformed with terror and excitement; then suddenly sits back on the sofa and goes into shrieks and peals of hysterical laughter. The noise is appalling.)

[After a moment there are voices and steps outside, and **GEORGE**, **CHARLES**, and **OCTAVIUS** enter almost simultaneously. **GEORGE** is dressed for dinner; but the other two have not yet finished their toilet.

GEORGE
Arabel!

CHARLES
For God's sake!

GEORGE
Arabel! What on earth—

OCTAVIUS
High-strikes! B-by Jove!

[**ARABEL** laughs on.

GEORGE (taking one of her hands and slapping it)
Stop that, Arabel! Stop it at once!

ARABEL (half gasping, half shrieking):
Married—gone—married—gone—

(She goes into another wild peal of laughter.)

GEORGE
Be quiet!

(Slaps her hand again.)

Fetch some water, someone . . .

OCTAVIUS
Eau-de-Cologne . . .

[**ALFRED**, **SEPTIMUS**, and **HENRY**, two of them dressed, the other without coat and collar, enter hurriedly.

ALFRED
What's the matter?

HENRY
Is Ba ill? Arabel!

ARABEL (gaspingly)
She's married—she's gone—married—gone . . .

[**HENRIETTA** enters in her cloak and bonnet. She stands for a moment, wide-eyed, taking in the scene.

Married and gone—Married and gone. . . .

(She moans and sobs.)

[Realisation begins to dawn on the brothers.

CHARLES
What does she mean? Where's Ba?

SEPTIMUS
Married and gone—she's mad!

GEORGE (taking **ARABEL** by the shoulder)
Arabel—what do you mean?

OCTAVIUS
Married . . . !

[**HENRIETTA** suddenly pushes them aside, seizes **ARABEL** by the shoulders and vigorously shakes her.

HENRIETTA
Arabel! Arabel! Pull yourself together at once! . . . Where's Ba? . . . Answer me! . . . Where's Ba?

ARABEL (gaspingly)

She—she's m-m-married Mr. Robert Browning. . . .

HENRIETTA (in a whisper)
Married . . .

[Consternation among the brothers and amazed exclamations: —"Married!"—"Married!"—"It can't be true!"—"Robert Browning!" —"Good God!" . . .

HENRIETTA (to **ARABEL**, who is still sobbing)
Where is she?

ARABEL
She—she's gone. . . . Those letters—She's written to—to all of us. . . . She—she's gone. . . .

[**OCTAVIUS** has pounced on the letters.

OCTAVIUS
F-for you.

(Hands a letter to **HENRIETTA**.)

[She tears it open and reads.

George—Henry—Alfred—Septimus—Charles.

[He hands them each a letter which is quickly torn open and read with muttered exclamations:—"Good God!"—"Impossible!"—"Married!" —"A week ago—"

GEORGE
Yes, she was married last Saturday.

OCTAVIUS (holding up a letter)
And this letter is for P-papa.

[A frightened silence falls on them. Only **HENRIETTA** looks before her with an inscrutable smile on her face.

ARABEL (in a shuddering whisper)
P-P-papa . . .

SEPTIMUS
Is he in?

GEORGE
Dressing for dinner.

OCTAVIUS
What's to be d-done?

HENRY
Someone must give him Ba's letter.

HENRIETTA (in a clear voice)
Let me. I should love to.

ARABEL (in a terrified whisper)
Oh, hush—hush . . .

[She points tremblingly to the door. They all hold their breath. In the pause one hears the sound of approaching footsteps. Then **BARRETT**, in evening dress, appears on the threshold. He looks at his assembled family in stern amazement. No one stirs.

BARRETT
What is the meaning of this?

[No one stirs or replies.

Who was making that hideous noise just now?

[No one stirs or replies.

Why are you gentlemen half-dressed?

[No one stirs or replies. A pause. Then sharply

Where is Elizabeth?

[A silence. He passes into the room. With a stifled cry, **ARABEL** rises and clings on to **HENRIETTA**'S arm.

Do you hear me? . . . (To **HENRIETTA**) Where is your sister?

HENRIETTA (freeing herself from **ARABEL** and picking up the letter):
She left you this letter.

BARRETT (without touching it, in a low voice, his face becoming a mask)
Left me. . . . What do you mean?

HENRIETTA
She left letters for all of us. This is yours.

[His eyes fixed on her face, he slowly takes the letter from her. He is about to open it when she suddenly seizes his arm.

(Passionately, entreatingly)

You must forgive her, Papa—you must forgive her—not for her sake—but for yours! I thought I hated you, but I don't. I pity you—I pity you. . . . And if you've any pity for yourself—forgive her. . . .

[He looks at her steadily for a moment; then puts her away from him. He opens and reads the letter. Nothing but his quickened breathing betrays the fury of emotions seething in him. His face, when at last he raises it from the letter, is a white mask. He stands motionless staring before him and mechanically folding and refolding the letter. He turns and walks to the window, and his gait somehow gives the impression that he is blind. He throws open the window and stands in front of it with his back to the room and his hands clasped behind him grasping the letter. The movement of his shoulders shows that he is breathing quickly and heavily. No one stirs.

BARRETT (half to himself, turning from the window)
Yes—yes. . . .Her dog. . . .

(A smile of indescribable ugliness flickers across his face.)
Yes—I'll have her dog. . . . Octavius.

OCTAVIUS
Sir?

BARRETT
Her dog must be destroyed. At once.

HENRIETTA
But—

BARRETT (slightly raising his voice)
You will take it to the vet—to-night. . . . You understand me? . . . To-night. (A pause.) You understand me?

OCTAVIUS (desperately)
I really d-don't see what the p-poor little beast has d-done to—

BARRETT (ominously)
You understand me?

HENRIETTA (vainly trying to control the triumph in her voice)
In her letter to me Ba writes that she has taken Flush with her. . . .

[A silence. **BARRETT** stands perfectly still, staring straight before him and mechanically tearing **ELIZABETH'S** letter into little pieces, which drop to his feet.

RUDOLF BESIER – A CONCISE BIBLIOGRAPHY

The Virgin Goddess (1906)
Don (1908)

Olive Latimer's Husband (1909)
The Foolish Virgin (prod. 1910-11)
Lady Patricia (1911)
Kipps (1912; with H. G. Wells, based on his book)
Her Country (prod. 1918)
Robin's Father (1918; with Hugh Walpole)
Secrets, 1922 (with May Edginton and filmed 1924, 1933)
A Lesson in Love (1922)
Prude's Fall (filmed 1924)
The Barretts of Wimpole Street (1930, Malvern; 1931 and filmed in 1934, 1957 and as a musical in 1964

Printed in Great Britain
by Amazon

37943770R00076